World-Class Risk Management

Norman Marks, CPA, CRMA

Contents

Foreword by Grant Purdy

People seek to achieve their overall goals by taking and implementing decisions against an environment that creates uncertainty. Quite simply, we are never sure quite how things will turn out when we make a decision; we always have incomplete and imperfect knowledge. Whether we call the effect this uncertainty has on our objectives "risk" or give it some other label doesn't change that reality.

On this basis, it makes sense that the purpose of managing this artificial concept we call "risk" is to improve decision-making so as to make it more likely that our subsequent actions will contribute as much as possible to the achievement of our objectives. It has no other valid role, whatsoever.

And it further makes sense that to achieve this purpose, the relevant sources of uncertainty associated with the proposed decision must first be detected by considering different scenarios and the nature and magnitude of the uncertainty and its implications explored and understood. Then, as necessary, our decision can be varied to ensure that the level and nature of the uncertainty we face are acceptable.

This is the process that we all intuitively follow when we make our decision to cross the road – we understand the risk, decide if it is OK and either cross now or delay until the risk is more acceptable.

It follows that, despite the general use of the term, risk is neither inherently good nor inherently bad. It is a neutral concept that is just a part of life and we must make of it what we can. However, if it is only viewed as bad, then this can lead us and our organisations to fail to expose themselves to the sorts of risk that are necessary for their objectives. Similarly, unless risk is always seen as being inseparably associated with objectives there will be confusion as to what is or is not risky. For example, there is a marked difference between how an approaching cyclone is viewed by a homeowner in its path and a company that repairs storm damage.

Of course, we should try to be more systematic and structured in the way we consider and tackle this thing we call risk, to counter some of the normal tendencies humans display when faced with a decision that will affect their future. Being more systematic allows us to:

- Challenge our assumptions and preconceptions before decisions are made, particularly whether the actions we decide to take will lead to success and will contribute to the achievement of our overall goals;

- Take appropriate actions to lower uncertainty that outcomes will be successful and that overall goals will be achieved;

- See early warning signs that the most important things (often called controls) we rely on for success and to achieve our objectives are not in place or are not fully effective, so that we can take early and pre-emptive action.

- Learn systematically from successes and failures in such a way that we can understand how to improve our decision-making next time and ensure the thing we reply on to be successful are in place actually work.

- Watch out for changes in our environment (internal and external) that might mean that risk has changed and we need to alter our decision or actions to ensure we are successful.

This process of risk management is, quite naturally, dynamic: it is triggered by the need to make a decision or review a previous decision because something of significance might have changed. It is not a static activity that is meant to occur because of a calendar or some committee meeting cycle that requires the generation of a report.

Unless this process is seen to and (only) used to support decisions, little real value is created. Worse still, these other uses (particularly if framed as *compliance*) distract from, dilute and confuse the natural risk management process.

The way I view risk and its management has evolved over the years and continues to change. I know that Norman's thoughts have also evolved and that while he and I come from totally different backgrounds and environments, we have both independently come to the conclusion that making things simpler makes them more obvious, logical and relevant.

However, it seems some others always want to make the simple and useful concepts and processes described above much more complex and opaque. Almost every month we hear of a new confection invented to explain the subject and which, in the process, confuses people even more. Many of these seem to fall within the category of solutions seeking problems and few pass muster on any test of intellectual rigour.

I'm pleased to say that Norman believes, like I do, that less is more and I'm delighted he has used his considerable experience in business to explain risk and its management from first principles, to challenge some of the logically inconsistent, complex and self-serving concepts that currently bedevil the practice and the profession.

Whether you are a manager, an assurance provider or a risk management professional, the way Norman has written this book and the good sense it contains should cause you to rethink your understanding of risk and how you go about recognising and responding to it.

Grant Purdy
Associate Director, Broadleaf Capital International
Melbourne, Australia.
April 2015

Introduction

What is "world-class" risk management?

There isn't any agreement on what the word 'risk'[1] means, so is there hope for agreement on what constitutes world-class risk management?

This book reflects my views, my opinion. It is based on my experiences as a risk officer and the executive responsible at various times for internal audit and information security. It has been shaped by my networking with and learning from luminaries in the field such as Grant Purdy in Australia; Jim DeLoach, Felix Kloman, and Arnold Schanfield in the US; Richard Anderson in the UK; John Fraser in Canada; Martin Davies in Singapore; Miriam Kraus in Germany; and many more[2]. I am also grateful to Alex Dali in France. Alex manages the excellent ISO 31000 Risk Management Standard discussion group on LinkedIn dedicated to the promotion of that standard; we have had a number of discussions about risk management and its integration into strategy-setting, decision-making, and more.

Over the years, I have written extensively about risk management in my two blogs (for The Institute of Internal Auditors and in my personal WordPress blog). I have reviewed, analyzed, criticized (unfortunately there is a lot of poor guidance to comment on) and shared my thoughts on surveys and thought leadership pieces from consulting firms. I have learned as I did so, not only from the authors of such pieces, but also from those who were kind enough to comment and engage in discussions of my posts.

I have been fortunate to be invited to present at a number of seminars and conferences around the world where I have seized the opportunity to extend my thinking through conversations with attendees as well as listening carefully to the messages from other presenters. I also served as a member of the U.S. technical advisory group that worked on the ISO[3] 31000:2009 risk management standard[4] and related guidance. I am

---

[1] A useful source of information on this topic ("what is risk") and other related issues is a 2011-2012 survey by the Global Institute for Risk Management Standards (G31000). It can be found at http://G31000.org/wp-content/uploads/2014/04/Global_Survey_ISO_31000_English.pdf.

[2] With apologies to those I have not mentioned.

[3] The International Organization for Standardization (ISO) is a worldwide federation of national standards bodies.

flattered to have been recognized for my risk management thought leadership by the Institute of Risk Management who made me an Honorary Fellow.

I have earned a reputation in some quarters as somebody who has problems with the COSO *Enterprise Risk Management – Integrated Framework*. There is some truth to that allegation as I have problems with the COSO document, as I point out in the book. However, the COSO product has valuable insights that I also share in the book and I respect many of the individuals who contributed to its development. I prefer the ISO 31000:2009 global risk management standard, but that is not perfect and I have commented on those imperfections as well[5].

I cannot give a lot of examples of world-class risk management because very few have achieved that distinction. A survey sponsored by COSO[6] in 2010[7] found that only 3.4% assessed their ERM program as "very mature". 17.4% said it was "somewhat mature". In 2015, the authors (from the ERM Initiative at North Carolina State University, led by Mark Beasley) published an update to the survey. *2015 Report on the Current State of Enterprise Risk Oversight: Update on Trends and Opportunities* paints a sad picture.

> "Results from all six years of our surveys continue to find that the approach to risk oversight [i.e., the management of risk – the authors are not talking about oversight by the board] in many organizations continues to be ad hoc and informal, with little recognized need for

---

[4] The full name is *Risk management — Principles and guidelines* and it was published in 2009

[5] Some of the imperfections are compensated for in national guidance. I especially like the Standards Australia HB436:2013, *Risk management guidelines: Companion to AS/NZS ISO 31000:2009.*

[6] The Committee of Sponsoring Organizations of the Treadway Commission (COSO) is a joint initiative of five organizations, the American Accounting Association, the American Institute of Public Accountants, Financial Executives International, The Association of Accountants and Financial Professionals in Business, and The Institute of Internal Auditors. They published the *Internal Control – Integrated Framework* in 1992 and updated it in 2013, and the *Enterprise Risk Management – Integrated Framework* in 2004.

[7] Current State of Enterprise Risk Oversight and Market Perceptions of COSO's ERM Framework

strengthened approaches to tracking and monitoring key risk exposures, especially emerging risks related to strategy. Even the large organizations, public companies, and financial services organizations admit that their risk management oversight processes are less than mature."

Professor Beasley and his team surveyed more than a thousand CFOs in the U.S. 45% reported they have "no enterprise-wide risk management in place" or are considering putting one in place; 30% have only a partial process, addressing some but not all risk areas; and just 25% have what they call a "complete [and] formal" enterprise-wide risk management process in place.

In addition, only 5% (extensively) and 15% (mostly) had positive answers to the question "To what extent do you believe the organization's risk management process is a proprietary strategic tool that provides unique competitive advantage?"

When Deloitte in 2013[8] asked executives how well risk management supported their ability to develop and execute on strategy, just 13% said "very well".

This is a key question and the answer is damning!

A report by FERMA[9], *Risk Management Benchmarking Survey 2014*, asked risk managers about their level of satisfaction with the remediation of ten risks, identified as "top risks". Only one, quality (design, safety, and liability of products and services) was rated high. Three were rated medium, and these included the critical areas of planning and execution of strategy, reputation and brand, and debt and cash flow. In the other six (political, compliance, competition, economic, market strategy, and human resources) risk managers assessed their satisfaction as low.

> **Key point**: Only 3.4% assessed their risk management system as "very mature" (COSO study); only 13% of executives said risk management supported their ability to develop and execute on strategy (Deloitte).

---

[8] *Exploring Strategic Risk*
[9] Federation of European Risk Management Associations

This survey was of risk managers, so it excluded organizations without an investment in risk professionals – where the maturity[10] of risk management is unlikely to be high.

Unfortunately, many seem to be satisfied with their risk management practices, apparently blind to their immaturity. Perhaps they don't appreciate how the effective consideration and management of uncertainty can lead to better decisions, improved outcomes, and enhanced long-term value to stakeholders. Perhaps they think of risk management as a regulatory burden, the responsibility of a specialist function and separate from day-to-day operation of the business, or a periodic review of a list of things that can go wrong. If so, I believe they are mistaken.

They are not asking the question Deloitte used so adroitly: does risk management support their organization's ability to develop and execute on strategy. When risk management is mature, let alone world-class, it will have a significant positive long-term effect on both the selection of strategy and its execution.

Ernst & Young (EY) studied compound corporate performance between 2004 and 2011 and reported[11] that "Companies in the top 20% of risk management maturity delivered three times the level of EBITDA than the bottom 20%" (20.3% compared to 7.4%). The top 20% similarly outperformed on revenue growth, 16.8% vs. 10.6%.

Aon[12] published their latest *Risk Maturity Index* in October, 2014. They believe that:

> "In today's ever-changing environment, the ability to anticipate opportunities and effectively understand and respond to risks is critical to the operational and financial well-being of organizations.

---

[10] Many see the implementation of risk management as something that takes time. Some talk about requiring five years or more. The concept of 'maturity' is that organizations are on a path from immature to fully developed, with increasing effectiveness as they develop. I talk about this later when I introduce maturity models. For now, 'maturity' is essentially equivalent to 'effectiveness'.

[11] *Turning risks into results*, 2011

[12] Aon describes themselves as "the leading global provider of risk management, insurance and reinsurance brokerage, and human resources solutions and outsourcing services".

This is increasingly important given that internal and external factors influencing organizational risk management practices continue to evolve."

Their research, in conjunction with The Wharton School of the University of Pennsylvania, indicated that organizations with what Aon assessed[13] as a highly mature risk management system[14] had (on average) "a 42% return on equity performance" compared to negative 23% for those with the lowest maturity programs. They found similar benefits from mature risk management when they looked at return on assets (+11% vs. -10%) and stock price volatility (34% lower).

Whether you believe these surveys and the results they portray or not, they merit our attention. My belief, which the surveys support, is that effective risk management enables more intelligent and informed decisions. Over the longer term, better decisions should result in better performance.

My hope is that this book, which explains what I believe world-class represents, will stimulate discussion and the stretching of practice beyond what many seem satisfied with today.

I know that many experienced and well-respected risk professionals will disagree with my views. For example, I believe it is more important to assess whether the overall level of risk to the achievement of each critical objectives is at an acceptable level that it is to assess whether individual risks are being managed as desired. (This is discussed in chapter 5.) Few organizations take that top-down approach and my belief (controversial as it may be) is that is one of the reasons risk management is very often not perceived by top executives as helping the organization develop and execute on strategy.

More controversial is my assertion that risk managers should apply their risk thinking to understand and manage the risks to the risk management system itself.

---

[13] Some believe Aon didn't go far enough when it identified the characteristics of 'highly mature' risk management systems.

[14] By "risk management system" I mean the way the organization manages risk – the combination of its framework (policies, mandate, resources, systems, etc.) and process. It is not intended to imply an automated system.

My hope is also that not only risk practitioners will benefit, but anybody who wants to excel as a board[15] member, executive, or decision-maker at any level.

After all, I believe that the management of risk is <u>not</u> something that can be left to risk officers.

No. The management of risk is an <u>essential</u> element in successful management.

It's about understanding what could or could not happen (i.e., uncertainty), the potential effect on the achievement of an organization's objectives (both positive and negative consequences), and taking actions to optimize outcomes.

Every manager should consider themselves as managers of risk. Managers and management teams will improve the likelihood and scale of their success when they integrate mature risk management practices into the setting of strategy and the daily management of their organization.

---

[15] In the book, I refer to the board of directors and members of the board. This is intended to refer equally to other oversight forms and structures, such as are found in government agencies and so on.

The language of risk

I said in the Introduction that there is no agreement on what the word "risk" means. I prefer the language used in the ISO 31000:2009 global risk management standard, which I will describe in Chapter 1. But that is not how "normal" people talk.

When I believe the point is made better in colloquial English, then that is the language I will use.

For example, I will use the expression "take a risk". To an ISO disciple, that is an expression that doesn't make a lot of sense. But in lay language it does – it means that we are willing to take an action and accept the consequences. The consultants at Ernst & Young talk about risk management helping you *take the right risks*, or to have the *confidence to take risks*. We know what they mean, and I use the words without apology because they communicate the point very well.

I have also used the phrase "risk management system" to describe how an organization manages risk. It is intended to include the framework, process, systems, organization, culture, and so on. Others may prefer to use this expression for an automated risk management solution, and the terms "risk management program", "approach", "process", and "framework" are sometimes used to describe what I refer to as the risk management system. None of these are perfect and I prefer "system".

Finally, I have used the word "risk" to describe not only the effect of uncertainty on objectives (the ISO definition of risk), but the situation that may give risk to risk. ISO 31000 defines a *risk source* as an "element which alone or in combination has the intrinsic potential to give rise to risk". But, common parlance is to use the word "risk" to describe these (just look at any list of so-called 'top risks') and so have I in this book.

My purpose in writing this book is to stimulate discussion of what world-class risk management is all about. I ask in advance for your forgiveness in using the language I think will work best and be readily understood, rather than always being technically correct.

Chapter 1: What is risk and why is risk management important?

As individuals, as well as leaders of organizations or teams, we have goals we want to achieve. Goals may vary from the desire to meet corporate revenue or profit targets to the need to get to our child's school in time to pick them up and take them home.

But our paths to those goals are uncertain. We cannot predict with certainty what will happen along the way.

Obstacles may appear that make it more difficult to achieve our goal. Equally, situations may arise that give us the opportunity to exceed our goal – whether that means that we beat our revenue targets or arrive at the school early.

Uncertainty lies between where we are and where we want to go.

If we want to do well in life, we need to understand what might happen, both good and bad, and take actions as appropriate.

As we prepare to drive to our child's school, we consider what might affect our trip, such as weather and traffic conditions, and plan accordingly. Once on the road, we are alert to dangers such as an erratic driver on our right or traffic merging ahead.

We are also watching to see whether changing lanes will let us take advantage of traffic conditions. For example, if we take a neighbor with us we can use the carpool lane to advantage.

Hopefully, we anticipate and prepare for such situations and should they occur we are ready to act.

That, quite simply, is risk management.

It's about understanding what might happen (uncertainty), assessing how it could affect the achievement of our objectives, and acting accordingly[16]. Let's illustrate with the simple example (at least simple on the surface) of the daily commute to work.

---

[16] Felix Kloman describes risk management in *The Fantods of Risk* (2008) as "a discipline for dealing with uncertainty".

Our objective is to arrive safely at work in time for our first meeting, which is scheduled to start at 8:30 a.m. We would prefer to arrive 10-20 minutes early (i.e., at around 8:10 a.m.) so we can drop our bag at our desk, grab a cup of coffee, and make our way to the conference room without having to hurry. We want to be at our best for the meeting, not rushing in at the last minute or late.

> **Key point**: Risk management is about understanding what might happen (uncertainty), assessing how it could affect the achievement of our objectives, and acting accordingly.

Our objective is to arrive safe and sound at 8:10 a.m. or earlier, ready to make a contribution to the meeting.

As diligent managers, we plan our trip. We think about what might happen and make reasonable preparations.

We know from experience that the drive to work normally takes between 20 and 30 minutes, but bad weather, traffic, or other incidents could delay us. Because these happen fairly often, we decide to allow 45 minutes for the journey and plan to leave home no later than 7:25 a.m.

The meeting is important, so last night we went to the gas station on the way home and filled up. We also checked the weather forecast and saw that fair weather was expected; however, the weather forecast is unreliable and we know we will have to check again in the morning. To ensure we wake up on time, we set the alarm clock for 6:45 a.m.

By the time we go to sleep, we have anticipated and prepared for a number of potential situations that might affect our morning commute. We allowed an extra 15 minutes of travel time for weather, traffic, or other delays; we also considered the possibility that we might run out of fuel and filled up the night before; there is a chance we might oversleep, so we set the alarm; and, while it is not a reliable indicator, we checked the weather forecast.

We considered a number of other uncertainties:

- Weather or traffic delays could hold us up by more than the extra 15 minutes we allowed. Based on prior experience, we believe 15 minutes is reasonable and know we have the "cushion" of the 20 minutes we set aside for getting ready for the meeting after we arrive at the office. We are willing to accept the chance that delays will be so severe that we are late.

- Although we addressed the chance of running out of fuel, other breakdowns might occur. However, we are assured by the fact that we have taken the car in for service regularly and accept the (hopefully minimal) risk that it will choose tomorrow morning to break down.

- The family may make demands on our time (such as the kids playing up instead of getting ready for school). While they are generally considerate when we tell them we have to hurry because we have an important meeting, we are willing to rely on our spouse to help as necessary. There is little we can do if our spouse falls sick (there is no indication as we go to bed) and accept the risk.

- There's a possibility that the alarm might fail to go off on time or that we might sleep through it. While we considered those events unlikely, we told our spouse that we have an important meeting and expect he/she will wake us if necessary; we are willing to accept the risk that he/she will forget or wake us too late.

- There's a slight chance that the meeting time or location will be changed. We checked our email and for phone messages before we went to bed and will check again in the morning. That's all we can do; if the meeting time is brought forward and we don't find out until it's too late for us to make it, there is nothing more we can reasonably do.

- We also haven't considered the possibility that traffic might be lighter than usual and allow us to arrive early. We are more concerned that we avoid getting in late so we defer until later deciding what we will do with our time if we are early.

We sleep well, knowing that we have thought about what might happen and have taken reasonable precautions. There is still a possibility that things could go wrong and cause us to be late, but we believe that risk is low and we are willing to take[17] it.

---

[17] Again, the risk technician might use the expression "accept the risk" instead of "take the risk".

In the morning, everything goes smoothly and as planned. We wake on time, check the weather outside (it is fine) and the radio for traffic conditions (none are reported that affect our route), and the family allows us to get ready and leave on time. There are no phone messages or emails saying that the meeting time or location has changed.

But our management of risk continues. There are many uncertain events and situations that can delay us or allow us to arrive early. We are going to keep our eyes and ears alert, monitoring possible sources of risk.

Throughout our journey, we monitor our vehicle for signs of a potential problem. We tune the radio to a news station that provides us with frequent traffic and weather alerts. We know the alternate routes should we see the traffic start to build on our regular route and stay in a position to exit the highway if needed.

We drive safely, staying far enough behind the car in front to stop should it brake without warning, and we will move out of the way should a vehicle start to tailgate us. There is still the possibility of another driver hitting us and we accept that risk, knowing that all we can do (unless we avoid the risk by staying home – and taking the risk of losing our job) is keep our eyes and ears attentive to what is happening around us.

We are alert to the opportunity to change lanes safely where it would allow us to travel faster, making sure that the risk we take when we change lanes is low, and that allows us to near our destination 15 minutes early.

Since we clearly will have time, we decide to stop at a local coffee shop to get some "real" coffee instead of relying on the machine at work.

As a result of our risk monitoring and ability to act when called for, we not only arrive safely on time, but with an excellent cup of coffee in hand.

We not only achieved but exceeded our objective!

What I just described is something that we do unconsciously all the time – and people have similarly been managing risk in their professional lives for many years without thinking of it as risk management.

The management of risk is not new. Every human, to some extent, considers what might happen and what it might lead to before making a decision or taking action.

The risk management discipline makes it a more reliable, systematic, and iterative activity.

It makes management and decision-making more effective by ensuring that we consider uncertainty, based on reliable current information, when we set objectives, goals and strategies - and then continue to manage that uncertainty as we execute against those objectives.

Risk management is not separate or distinct from management of the organization: it is essential to effective management. It is a critical element of decision-making and the optimization of performance and value creation.

In May, 2015, the International Federation of Accountants (IFAC) published *From Bolt-on to Built-in: Managing Risk as an Integral Part of Managing an Organization*[18]. The thought paper agreed on this point, saying that "it is time to recognize that managing risk and establishing effective control form natural parts of an organization's system of management that is primarily concerned with setting and achieving its objectives. Effective risk management and internal control, if properly implemented as an integral part of managing an organization, is cost effective and requires less effort than dealing with the consequences of a detrimental event. It also generates value from the benefits gained through identified and realized opportunities".

IFAC continued:

> "Risk management should never be implemented in isolation; it should always be fully integrated into the organization's overall system of management. This system should include the organization's processes for good governance, including those for strategy and planning, making decisions in operations, monitoring, reporting, and establishing accountability."

Let's take this discussion to the next level by defining some terms. The first term we need to define is "risk" itself.

---

[18] Available at http://www.ifac.org/publications-resources/bolt-built.

Defining Risk

The common English meaning of "risk" is something bad that may interfere with our ability to succeed. "Taking a risk" means that we are accepting[19] the possibility that something bad might happen, hopefully because we believe the likelihood is low and the potential consequences minimal.

> **Key point**: Risk management is not separate or distinct from management of the organization: it is essential to effective management. It is a critical element of decision-making and the optimization of performance and value creation.

But the uncertainty before us, between where we stand and where we want to go, holds not only the possibility of bad but of good things happening.

I like the definition of risk in the global risk management standard from the *International organization for Standardization* (ISO), *31000:2009 Risk management - Principles and guidelines*. They define risk as "the effect of uncertainty on objectives".

This definition encompasses both the potential positive and negative effects of uncertainty, although most of us concentrate on what might go wrong when we talk about risk management.

Felix Kloman similarly defines risk[20] without limiting it to adverse effects: "a measure of the probable likelihood, consequences, and timing of a future event".

However, many prefer to talk about "risk" as limited to the negative effect of uncertainty and "opportunity" as the positive effect. This is the position taken by COSO[21] in its 2004 *Enterprise Risk Management - Integrated Framework*:

> "Events can have negative impact, positive impact, or both. Events with a negative impact represent risks, which can prevent value creation or erode existing value. Events with positive impact may offset negative impacts or represent opportunities. Opportunities are

---

[19] I like to think of this as exposing yourself to the possibility of an adverse outcome, either because you hope for reward or it is the 'least bad' alternative. For example, we 'take a risk' every time we breathe because of the possibility that we inhale germs, etc. However, the alternative to breathing is a poor one.
[20] *Fantods of Risk*
[21] Committee of Sponsoring Organizations of the Treadway Committee

the possibility that an event will occur and positively affect the achievement of objectives, supporting value creation or preservation."

They also say this about uncertainty and risk management

"Uncertainty presents both risk and opportunity, with the potential to erode or enhance value. Enterprise risk management enables management to effectively deal with uncertainty and associated risk and opportunity, enhancing the capacity to build value."

The trouble with this is that while COSO ERM explains that risk management[22] encompasses the management of both risk and opportunity, their guidance concentrates on the negative and this has extended to how risk management is practiced in most organizations. In other words, the potential positive effect of uncertainty is ignored[23,24].

This was reinforced when I attended a presentation by Anette Mikes; at the time she was an Assistant Professor at Harvard Business School where she researched and wrote about risk management[25]. She shared how she had met with the chief risk officer of Lego, the privately-held Danish toy company. He told her about an upcoming new product launch in Eastern Europe and how the risk assessment process had identified as a risk the possibility that demand for the new products would be overwhelming, leading to a failure to satisfy customer demand, in turn leading to customer dissatisfaction and the potential to impair sales in the future.

Professor Mikes was pleased that the disciplined process followed at Lego had identified the possibility that an apparently positive situation (greater than expected demand) could have a negative effect on the organization. I agree that the risk function did well to identify that an inability to satisfy customer demand might have long-lasting adverse impacts.

---

[22] COSO uses the term "enterprise risk management", but I prefer the simpler "risk management" and will use that term in this book.

[23] In addition, I am concerned with the idea that positive effects (opportunities in COSO language) may offset adverse effects (risks). I discuss this further in the chapter on risk assessment.

[24] Another often overlooked issue is that a single event can have multiple consequences, some of which may be positive and others negative.

[25] Professor Mikes is now a member of the Business and Economics Faculty at the University of Lausanne, where she continues her work on risk management.

But I was disappointed to hear that, according to Professor Mikes[26], the response by Lego focused only on treating the negative effects and not exploiting the opportunity presented by greater than projected demand.

When Professor Mikes talked about the actions Lego was taking to address the possibility that demand would exceed forecast, she didn't mention the company readying manufacturing to ramp up in response, whether inventories earmarked for other locations might be shipped to Eastern Europe, or if the company was prepared to discontinue or limit discounts to retailers buying in bulk. Instead, the discussion was about the steps management might take to address customer complaints.

I would have preferred a much richer and broader discussion about what might happen. For example, a risk manager (RM) might meet with operating management (OM) and the conversation might go along these lines:

RM: What is the forecast demand for our new product in this market?

OM: 2 million units in the first 3 months.

RM: What is your confidence level that you will be within a few percentage points of that number? What is the likelihood of 2 million?

OM: Good question; we think there is a 75% likelihood we will hit 2 million, 10% that it will fall short, and 15% that it will be significantly more.

RM: OK. Let's first take the 10% probability that it will fall short. Have you done everything within reason, such as increased advertising or price discounts, to minimize the likelihood of missing the 2 million target?

OM: I think so. There is always more, but the cost outweighs the potential benefit.

RM: So there is a 10% likelihood that you will miss your target. Can I assume you have done everything reasonable to keep the shortfall as small as possible? What do you expect the shortfall to be, if it arises?

---

[26] The CRO of Lego attended the First international ISO 31000 conference in 2012 run by Alex Dali, President of G31000. Mr. Dali recalls that an assistant to the CRO said that his program was "embedded in decision-making and was a leverage for exploiting opportunities".

OM: Yes, I think we have done everything we should as part of our efforts to increase the likelihood of achieving the 2 million target. We believe there is a 10% likelihood of falling short by no more than 200,000. Before you ask, we have plans in place to move those 200,000 units to another market quite quickly should we need. We thought about offering additional discounts to clear the excess inventory but decided that it would lead to price erosion that would be more harmful than incurring the costs of moving inventory.

RM: That's interesting. Have you considered moving inventory to the area in stages, so that if demand is less than expected the cost of moving excess inventory would be reduced?

OM: That's a good idea. I will talk to our logistics staff and have them explore the pros and cons of moving the inventory in stages.

RM: Is there anything else you could do to minimize the negative impact of missing the target? Apart from reduced sales, where else would the company be affected?

OM: Well, there would be impacts on our financial results and on cash flow. Let me talk to our finance and treasury people to see if they have planned how they would handle the revenue shortfall. In fact, I would like you to come with me when we meet. As I think about it, perhaps we should also talk to the investor relations team, as they might have to handle press or investor questions.

RM: Certainly, I would be happy to join you. These situations often affect a number of different departments. For example, would the people managing our warehouses need to have plans should we end up with more inventory than planned and have to move it? Won't manufacturing have to adjust their plans because the 200,000 units will be diverted from Eastern Europe instead of manufactured for the other markets?

OM: You raise some good points; perhaps we should have a much larger discussion with all of these people involved.

RM: I think that would be an excellent idea. Let's put a list together of all potentially affected departments before we close our meeting and then I would appreciate your inviting them to our meeting. Let's call it a risk workshop.

OM: I would be happy to do that.

RM: But there's a couple of other questions on my mind. First, if demand fails to hit the target, would you need to change your forecasts for the other markets? Then, will you be able to tell quickly whether you are going to hit the target, exceed it, or fall short?

.......the conversation continues, focusing on how the company will address a failure to hit the forecast demand. Then:

RM: OK, let's switch the subject to the possibility that demand may actually outstrip the forecast. You said that there was a 15% chance of that. How great could the demand be?

OM: We think there is a 10% chance that we will hit 2,250,000 and a 5% chance of 2,500,000.

RM: So let's consider what effect either of those would have. Are there potential downsides?

OM: Yes. Customers could be upset that the product is not available and the social media might pick up on it. In the worst case, customers might decide not to even try to purchase our product because they think it will be sold out. There might also be talk that there was a management failure to plan the product release effectively and that might hurt our reputation and future sales. As I think about it, that customer concern could spread outside this particular market to Western Europe.

RM: Have you discussed this with all the departments that might be affected, including the managers responsible for manufacturing and marketing for the other markets – and investor relations, as you pointed out?

OM: I guess we can add this to the agenda for the risk workshop.

RM: Yes. And let's also discuss in the workshop how we can take *advantage* of the increased demand. For example, we will need to find out whether this could be an indication that demand will be more than forecast in the other regions, and whether total demand will be higher than expected or only reflects people buying earlier than we thought. There might even be an opportunity to have higher prices when we release the product in France and Germany (they are the next markets targeted, I think).

OM: It sounds like the risk workshop is something we need to organize very quickly if we are to manage any downside and take advantage of potential upsides. Thanks for suggesting it!

Effective decision-making, and I suggest effective risk management, is about optimizing outcomes. It's not only about achieving objectives (our desired outcome) by managing adverse risks in our path; it's about increasing the likelihood and extent of our success.

As I noted earlier, in their latest *2014 Risk Maturity Index*, Aon reported that:

> "In today's ever-changing environment, the ability to anticipate opportunities and effectively understand and respond to risks is critical to the operational and financial well-being of organizations. This is increasingly important given that internal and external factors influencing organizational risk management practices continue to evolve."

I can understand why the regulators (more on this later) focus on the downside as they are all about protecting the interests of the stakeholders. They are concerned about management exposing the company to too much risk. Their guidance is not intended to lead management to take more downside risk, even when doing so is justified by the ability to manage any adverse effect[27] and the potential for reward.

But, we must remember that it is essential that management take *enough* risk! If they take no risk, the organization will fail. So risk management is about taking the **right** risks for the organization at desired levels, balancing the opportunities on the upside and the potential for harm on the downside.

---

[27] Some refer to this as "risk capacity," a term used more often when considering financial risk. In a 2010 report, *It's all about balance*, Accenture proposed that that the key to successful risk management was balancing your risk appetite against your risk-bearing capacity. They went on to define the latter as: "a measure of a company's resiliency and agility—an estimate of its ability to take on new opportunities, as well as the scope and type of economic shocks it can bear without a serious decline in its operational effectiveness." Deloitte also uses the term, defining it as "the maximum level of risk at which a firm can operate while remaining within constraints implied by capital and funding needs and its obligations to stakeholders".

The IFAC thought paper referenced earlier identified one of the top serious flaws in risk management practices as:

> Treating **risk as only negative** and overlooking the idea that organizations need to take risks in pursuit of their objectives. Effective risk management enables an organization to exploit opportunities and take on additional risk while staying in control and, thereby, creating and preserving value.

So let's not limit our discussion of risk management to the negative. Instead, let's talk about how we can and should understand the uncertainty between where we are and where we want to go so that we can take the right risks and optimize outcomes: the achievement of our objectives[28].

When this is done in a systematic and disciplined way, the quality of our decisions and results will improve.

> **Key point**: It is essential that management take *enough* risk! If they take no risk, the organization will fail. So risk management is about taking the **right** risks for the organization at desired levels, balancing the opportunities on the upside and the potential for harm on the downside.

COSO recognizes that when organizations include the consideration of uncertainty when they set strategies and objectives to create value, make decisions and manage the organization, and when they monitor performance and adjust as necessary, they are more likely to succeed.

They continue:

> "   and avoid pitfalls and surprises along the way."

COSO tells us that effective risk management gives us "a greater likelihood of achieving business objectives". It also enables "more informed risk-taking and decision-making".

They define risk management:

---

[28] I like the way uncertainty is described in Standards Australia HB 436, *Risk Management Guidelines: Companion to AS/NZS ISO 31000:2009* – "Organisations of all kinds face internal and external factors and influences that make it uncertain whether, when, and the extent to which, they will achieve or exceed their objectives."

"Enterprise risk management is a process, effected by an entity's board of directors, management and other personnel, applied in strategy setting and across the enterprise, designed to identify potential events that may affect the entity, and manage risk to be within its risk appetite, to provide reasonable assurance regarding the achievement of entity objectives".

Key to this definition is "risk appetite", which COSO defines as follows:

"Risk appetite is the amount of risk, on a broad level, an organization is willing to accept in pursuit of value. Each organization pursues various objectives to add value and should broadly understand the risk it is willing to undertake in doing so."

When people talk about risk appetite, they invariably think only about the need for risk not to exceed the risk appetite of the organization. However, in the risk appetite discussion later in this book, I will suggest that this is insufficient. It will prevent managers from taking too much risk, but it will not guide them to take *enough* risk.

I prefer to think of risk appetite as a range: the low end is the minimum level of risk you are willing to take because you have the ability to accept the risk, and recognize that taking risk is essential to achieving your objective. The high end is the maximum level of risk you can afford to take.

The global standard for risk management from the *International organization for Standardization* (ISO) is their *31000:2009 Risk management - Principles and guidelines*[29]. The *National Standards Authority of Ireland* published implementation guidance for ISO 31000:2009 in which they said:

"The purpose of managing risk is to increase the likelihood of an organization achieving its objectives by being in a position to manage threats and adverse situations and being ready to take advantage of opportunities that may arise."

The accounting and consulting firm, Ernst & Young, expresses the value of risk management eloquently.

---

[29] The ISO definition of risk management is less than helpful: "coordinated activities to direct and control an organization with regard to risk".

"Effective risk management gives you the confidence to take risks."

I really like this. It reminds us that informed risk management is not about avoiding or treating risks. It's about taking the **right** risks!

When you have an effective risk management system, you have confidence that you have identified, analyzed, and evaluated the uncertainties between where you are and where you want to go. You know which risks you should take and which you should not. You also have confidence that should new risks appear, or existing risks change, you can respond promptly and effectively.

When you don't have this information, you have to be more cautious, but when you have confidence in your risk management system you can run the business at the desired speed[30] and take the right risks.

If we don't take risks we will die. To succeed in life or in business, we need to take the right risks among all those available to us.

The EY study I referenced earlier is useful to repeat: organizations with mature risk management outperform their peers when it comes to revenue growth and earnings.

In their *2011 Global Risk Management Study*, Accenture had a lot to say on this subject:

> "Beyond the immediate pressures of global markets, more demanding customers and dramatic industry change is a growing recognition that companies have an opportunity to drive competitive advantage from their risk management capabilities, enabling long-term profitable growth and sustained future profitability.

> "This means that risk management at the top-performing companies is now more closely integrated with strategic planning and is conducted proactively, with an eye on how such capabilities might help a company move into new markets faster or pursue other evolving growth strategies."

They quoted the Chief Risk Officer of a global reinsurance company as saying that the firm's enterprise risk management framework "is really tailored to the company to turn it into a competitive advantage."

---

[30] Our world is accelerating and decisions have to be made at increasing speed.

But at the same time, Deloitte is telling us (in the 2013 study mentioned above) that very few have risk management systems that satisfactorily contribute to the achievement of strategies and objectives.

Let's examine why.

Perhaps one of the reasons is that the guidance many rely on as they implement risk management has room for improvement.

Chapter 2: Effective risk management

There are two primary sets of guidance[31] for risk management: COSO's 2004[32] *Enterprise Risk Management – Integrated Framework* (COSO) and the ISO 2009[33] International Standard[34], *Risk management — Principles and guidelines* (ISO 31000:2009).

Both COSO and ISO provide guidance on what constitutes *effective* risk management.

The COSO approach is to explain that risk management "consists of eight interrelated components", which they describe in their Framework. They go on to say that:

> "Determining whether an entity's enterprise risk management is "effective" is a judgment resulting from an assessment of whether the eight components are present and functioning effectively. Thus, the components are also criteria for effective enterprise risk management. For the components to be present and functioning properly there can be no material weaknesses, and risk needs to have been brought within the entity's risk appetite."

I will accept that if all the COSO components are perfect, then risk management is almost certainly going to be effective.

But COSO asserts that the determination of whether they are *perfect* is based on the quality of the results. COSO says that: "For the components to be present and functioning properly there can be no material weaknesses, and risk needs to have been brought within the entity's risk appetite."

This is saying that risk management is effective when the components are present and functioning, and that is achieved when risk management is effective.

---

[31] There are a number of other useful authoritative publications, the best of which (in my opinion) are centered around ISO 31000:2009. The Standards Australia publication, *HB436: Risk management guidelines – Companion to ISO 31000:2009* merits attention.

[32] In October 2014, COSO announced a project to update the ERM Framework.

[33] ISO has a project underway that is expected to result in some changes to the standard.

[34] The ISO risk management standard is not intended, in contrast to other ISO standards, to be used as a basis for certification.

I don't find that helpful.

I prefer the approach in ISO 31000:2009, where the determination of whether risk management is effective is (to a large degree) based on whether it achieves certain results rather than form.

The ISO 31000 Risk Management Principles

ISO 31000:2009 says that risk management is effective when "an organization at all levels complies with" (achieves) a number of principles:

1: Risk management creates and protects value.

2: Risk management is an integral part of all organizational processes.

3: Risk management is part of decision making.

4: Risk management explicitly addresses uncertainty.

5: Risk management is systematic, structured and timely.

6: Risk management is based on the best available information.

7: Risk management is tailored.

8: Risk management takes human and cultural factors into account.

9: Risk management is transparent and inclusive.

10: Risk management is dynamic, iterative and responsive to change.

11: Risk management facilitates continual improvement of the organization.

The Institute of Risk Management (IRM) summarized this in a useful fashion[35]:

"Risk management is a process that is under-pinned by a set of principles. Also, it needs to be supported by a structure that is appropriate to the organisation and its external environment or context. A successful risk management initiative should be proportionate to the level of risk in the organisation (as related to the size, nature and complexity of the organisation), aligned with other

---

[35] *A structured approach to Enterprise Risk Management and the requirements of ISO 31000*, AIRMIC, Alarm, IRM: 2010 (with permission)

corporate activities, comprehensive in its scope, embedded into routine activities and dynamic by being responsive to changing circumstances."

I believe the effectiveness of risk management should be assessed based on whether it delivers the desired results[36] – reliable, useful and timely information that enables better decisions. (See chapter 18 for a discussion of world-class risk management: a step up from effective.)

While the ISO principles are important and a strong argument can be made that effective risk management requires that they are all achieved, I believe we need to ensure that risk management is helping managers and the board set and achieve

> **Key point**: The effectiveness of risk management should be assessed based on whether it delivers the desired results – reliable, useful and timely information that enables better decisions.

effective strategies for the creation of value for their stakeholders. Another way of saying this is that risk management enables management across the organization and the board to make intelligent decisions and take the right risks. I will discuss this in more detail later.

Each of the eleven principles merits our attention.

1. <u>Risk management creates and protects value</u>

The key here is the recognition that risk management is not a purely defensive activity. It is not just about preventing bad things happening that may destroy value (such as frauds, compliance failures, losses from natural disasters, etc.) but includes seizing opportunities that may present themselves.

It is not often acknowledged, but COSO says much the same (as previously quoted):

> "Events can have negative impact, positive impact, or both. Events with a negative impact represent risks, which can prevent value

---

[36] Some believe that if events unfold in a way that is consistent with the risk assessment, risk management is effective. But I don't hold to that view: there is too much 'luck' involved. Instead, I assess risk management as effective when decision-makers assert that it helps them make better decisions.

creation or erode existing value. Events with positive impact may offset negative impacts or represent opportunities. Opportunities are the possibility that an event will occur and positively affect the achievement of objectives, supporting value creation or preservation. Management channels opportunities back to its strategy or objective-setting processes, formulating plans to seize the opportunities."

Effective risk management is not focused only on managing the potentially negative effect of uncertainty on the achievement of objectives, but includes managing potential positive effects - seizing opportunities as they arise.

It is about achieving and even surpassing objectives.

2. Risk management is an integral part of all organizational processes

This principle is about the need for risk management to be part of how you run the business; it should not be set up as a silo operation. The principle recognizes that the consideration of risk needs to be included in daily business activities such as vendor selection, capital expenditure approvals, hiring of employees, acquisitions, and more.

COSO's *Embracing Enterprise Risk Management: Practical Approaches for Getting Started* echoes this point:

"As articulated in COSO's ERM definition, enterprise risk management is a process that is applied across the organization. It is a management process, ultimately owned by the chief executive officer and involves people at every level of the organization. The comprehensive nature of the ERM process and its pervasiveness across the organization and its people provides the basis for its effectiveness.

"ERM cannot be viewed or implemented as a stand-alone staff function or unit outside of the organization's core business processes. In some companies and industries, such as large banks, it is common to see a dedicated enterprise risk management unit to support the overall ERM effort including establishing ERM policies and practices for their business units. However, because ERM is a process, organizations may or may not decide that they need dedicated, stand-alone support for their ERM activities.

"Whether a risk management unit exists or not, a key to success is linking or embedding the ERM process into its core business processes and structures of the organization. Some organizations, for example, have expanded their strategic plans and budgeting processes to include the identification and discussion of the risks related to their plans and budgets."

One important implication of this is that the consideration of risk cannot be assigned to a risk management function. Decisions that create or modify risk are being made across the organization all the time, and there simply is no way to involve a risk officer in every decision. It is essential that the managers making the decisions and taking the risks understand how to do so. It is essential, in other words, for every manager to be a risk professional.

What I mean by that is that every decision-maker needs to be trained in risk management practices and methods. Ideally, the effective management of risk should be a core requirement in MBA and other management (and board) training programs.

3: Risk management is part of decision making

This is an extension of the prior principle[37]. If a decision is to be made effectively, the decision-maker has to consider all options – what might happen with each option and how would situations be handled.

Managers have been considering "what might happen" as they make decisions for as long as there have been decisions to be made[38]. Risk management brings a more systematic and disciplined process to the consideration of "what might happen" and how that might affect the achievement of objectives.

Again, every decision-maker needs to be a risk professional: someone whose job includes managing risk.

---

[37] ...and probably should have been included in it rather than being identified as separate principles.
[38] Adam and Eve might have benefitted from a more disciplined approach before making their decision to eat that apple!

4: Risk management explicitly addresses uncertainty

The ISO standard doesn't really explain this principle beyond saying that risk management is about understanding and addressing uncertainty[39]. My interpretation is that risk management should consider everything that is uncertain between where you are and where you want to go. People tend to think about all the things that could go wrong, but not often enough think about the assumptions they have made – what needs to go right. I will expand on this later.

5: Risk management is systematic, structured and timely

As I mentioned earlier, managers have always considered risk when they are making decisions. The value of risk management is that it brings discipline to the exercise.

The last word of the principles, "timely", is important: risk should not be considered *after* the decision has been made. It has to be an integral part of the decision-making process. That means that the person making the risk has to be trained in effective risk management, or advised by somebody who is, at the time of the decision.

All too often, strategies and objectives are set and only then is the risk officer tasked with helping management identify and assess related risks.

6: Risk management is based on the best available information

Simple but important: decisions are better when all the relevant information is considered, and that information needs to be reliable, current, timely, complete, and clear. The same applies to the management of risk. When determining whether the risk is at an acceptable level and what action to take, if any, it is essential that information about the risk and treatment options be as reliable as possible.

---

[39] ISO 31000:2009 provides a definition of uncertainty, but it doesn't really add much clarity in my opinion: "Uncertainty is the state, even partial, of deficiency of information related to, understanding or knowledge of an event, its consequence, or likelihood".

In a dynamic world, where business conditions change at speed, a slow risk management process that only looks at risk on an occasional basis is highly likely to result in ineffective management of those risks.

7: Risk management is tailored

The ISO standard includes a process diagram that explains in broad strokes the steps taken in a risk management process. However, the processes and policies that an organization should implement must be tailored to fit the specific circumstances and needs of the organization.

The typical organization has multiple risk management processes. The IT, treasury, procurement, capital allocation, strategy development, and other functions need to integrate the consideration of risk into how they run their part of the business (as discussed later). The management of risk (including the policies, standards, and organization that enable it[40]) needs to be tailored to suit the nature of the risks and decisions that need to be made. So there is not, or at least should not be, one risk management process[41]. (One danger of talking about a single risk management process is that it may lead people to believe that a centralized risk management process, separate from how strategies are set and the business is run, is desirable. Nothing could be further from the truth. The management of risk has to be embedded into daily decision-making and the operation of the business.)

However, when there are multiple risk management processes, it is essential that they work together. Senior management and the board need information on how risks to organizational objectives are being handled across the organization, especially considering that multiple departments might be responsible for addressing only a portion of a risk, and the action of one area may impact performance in one or more other areas.

---

[40] Part of what ISO 31000:2009 refers to as the risk management framework.

[41] ISO 31000 advocates assert there is only one risk management process. It is true that all risk management processes follow the same basic structure, with the same essential steps, but I find it confusing to talk about one risk management process when many business processes manage risk. As Jim DeLoach told me, it may be better to say that ISO 31000:2009 describes a common process that is integrated into or adapted by different operating units and functions.

Risk management needs to be tailored to meet the needs of the business, considering such factors as whether decision-making is centralized or decentralized (and variations in between those extremes), fast-moving and entrepreneurial in a dynamic environment or cautious in a static and highly regulated compliance environment, and so on. (In chapter 17, I will cover this and the topic of matching the speed of risk management to the speed of risk.)

8: Risk management takes human and cultural factors into account

I see a couple of aspects to this principle.

First, the design of the risk management system (how it is tailored) has to take into account the culture of the organization and the society in which it operates – including how decisions are made and how governance is performed. "Every organization's culture has strengths and limitations which must be taken into account when tailoring risk management."[42] Culture is the topic of a discussion in chapter 10.

Second, people make decisions and risk management needs to take this into account. Individuals have bias based on their prior experience and motivations (such as wanting things to be a certain way), which can affect how they identify, analyze, evaluate, and then act to address risks (this risk is discussed in chapter 17).

People also absorb information in different ways, with some requiring more detail than others. For example, some prefer an in-person briefing while others want a detailed paper.

Risk management has to accommodate these different needs for information if it is to be effective and enable decision-makers to make informed, risk-intelligent[43] decisions.

9: Risk management is transparent and inclusive

The text of ISO 31000:2009 talks about the need to involve and inform stakeholders, and decision-makers in particular, so that risk management

---

[42] This is a quote from ISO 31000:2009.
[43] I like this term, coined by Deloitte for the *Risk-Intelligent* series of thought leadership papers, several of which are excellent.

remains relevant and up-to-date. It also says that the interests of stakeholders should be represented in defining risk criteria (which are used to determine whether a risk is acceptable or not).

In 2014, ISO published *TR 31004: Risk Management- Guidance for the Implementation of ISO 31000*[44]. In its Annex B, the publication provided a little (emphasis on 'little') explanation for the principle. It talks about the need for stakeholders in risk management (those relying on its performance) to be sufficiently involved that they trust its results. At the same time, the need to protect confidential information must be respected.

Our world seems obsessed by the word "transparent". Reporters and political analysts talk about the need for transparency in every corner of governance. I wonder whether an element of this invaded the writing of this principle.

In any event, there is truth that managers and employees must trust the guidance that comes to them in making decisions and doing their jobs. They need to trust that when they are told to do things a certain way, which will affect their work and potentially their job performance and compensation, that there are good reasons for that guidance and instruction.

If they distrust the guidance and see it as an obstacle to their own interests, they may bypass or ignore it.

There is also truth that those affected most by guidance, such as risk criteria, are likely to have a great deal of information that should be considered in setting the guidance.

Guidance and instruction that is perceived as arbitrary and divorced from the realities of the work environment is unlikely to be followed.

10: <u>Risk management is dynamic, iterative and responsive to change</u>

In many ways, this is the most important principle in ISO 31000.

The world we live and work in is dynamic. The business environment is changing constantly and with increasing speed, even without

---

[44] I was one of the members of the US Technical Advisory Group that commented on and contributed to the development of ISO TR 31004:2014.

consideration of the impact of political, regulatory, and environmental change (such as floods in Thailand, New York, and England, or earthquakes and tsunamis in Japan and elsewhere).

This means that the risks to the achievement of our objectives are also changing constantly and with increasing speed.

Our ability to understand, analyze, and react to those changes must keep up.

That in turn means that our capability to detect new or changed risks must be designed to provide the information we need to be able to respond in a timely fashion.

It also means that we need to be able to adapt, making new decisions or revising earlier ones, as necessary.

The organization needs to be sufficiently agile to react to change promptly, either to reduce the extent and likelihood of potential damage or to seize an advantage before it disappears.

The last phrase in the principle, "responsive to change", reinforces that need – the ability to respond at speed.

The middle phrase, "iterative", speaks to a related need for the risk management system to be disciplined, systematic, and consistent.

The monitoring implied by the need to be able to know when there are changes, has to be consistent and disciplined if it is to be effective. A casual look, even if regular, is unlikely to be reliable.

I say this is "the most important principle" because the majority of organizations only have a periodic risk management process. They assess and discuss the condition of a limited number of risks (the top risks in a 'risk register') once a quarter or even less frequently.

This is demonstrably ineffective in a dynamic world.

Risk management must operate at the speed of the business and its environment.

11: Risk management facilitates continual improvement and enhancement of the organization

It is interesting that ISO 31000 and the guidance in TR 31004 both focus on the continued improvement of risk management. This is clearly important: every activity and process should be reviewed on a regular basis to see if it can be improved.

But I see this more broadly.

When a risk level rises, it may be because the way that the organization handles an activity or situation is no longer as effective as desired. There may have been some degradation of performance of related controls, or the volume or complexity of transactions that need to be handled may have increased. Either way, action is required.

If we take the example of higher compliance risk due to changes in regulations, the action may be to increase management monitoring or an upgraded software solution. Either qualifies as an "enhancement of the organization".

So, risk management enables us to detect when changes are needed in people, process, organization, or systems, and act accordingly.

Does this merit being one of the key principles for the effective management of risk, when every process and activity should be reviewed on a regular basis and upgraded as necessary? I would not have included it.

Risk Management Principles – Revisited

We have now reviewed the eleven principles.

My view is that while all eleven are going to be present to a degree when you have a mature and effective risk management system, they don't really describe what makes a risk management system effective – let alone world-class.

A mature program almost certainly achieves all eleven principles[45]. But, I am not persuaded that achieving all eleven means that your program is necessarily effective.

---

[45] ISO 31000:2009 says that all eleven principles must be satisfied for an

My problem is that the principles seem to set a low bar. For example, let's look at Principle #1: "Risk management creates and protects value". Nothing is said about how much value is enough. Shouldn't an effective risk management system come close to optimizing value, not just "creating and protecting value"?

If we look at Principle #3, it says: "Risk management is part of decision making". Shouldn't the consideration of risk be an essential and integral part of decision-making?

If I ruled the world and could change the ISO 31000:2009 principles, I would. Here are the ISO principles and my version compared.

Principles in ISO 31000:2009	Norman's Revised Principles
1: Risk management creates and protects value.	1: Risk management enables management to make intelligent decisions when setting strategy, making decisions, and in the daily management of the organization. It provides reasonable assurance that performance will be optimized, objectives achieved, and desired levels of value delivered to stakeholders.
2: Risk management is an integral part of the organizational procedure.	Not needed as I would include it in #1.
3: Risk management is part of decision making.	Not needed as I would include it in #1.

---

organization's approach to managing risk to be effective.

Principles in ISO 31000:2009	Norman's Revised Principles
4: Risk management explicitly addresses uncertainty.	2: Risk management provides decision-makers with reliable, current, timely, and actionable information about the uncertainty that might affect the achievement of objectives.
5: Risk management is systematic, structured and timely.	3: Risk management is systematic and structured. (Timeliness is covered in my #2.)
6: Risk management is based on the best available information.	Not needed, covered by my #2
7: Risk management is tailored.	4: Risk management is tailored to the needs of the organization and updated/upgraded as needed. This takes into account the culture of the organization, including how decisions are made, and the need to monitor the program itself and continually improve it.
8: Risk management takes human and cultural factors into account.	5: Risk management takes human factors (that may present the possibility failures to properly identify, analyze, evaluate or treat risks) into consideration and provides reasonable assurance they are overcome.
9: Risk management is transparent and inclusive.	I would not include this as a principle, as explained earlier.
10: Risk management is dynamic, iterative and responsive to change.	6: Risk management is dynamic, iterative and responsive to change.

Principles in ISO 31000:2009	Norman's Revised Principles
11: Risk management facilitates continual improvement and enhancement of the organization.	I would not include this as a principle. It is covered by my #4 and management should always be looking to continually improve, so this is not a distinguishing feature of risk management.

So, I have reduced the list to six instead of eleven principles, re-ordered as follows:

1: Risk management enables management to make intelligent decisions when setting strategy, planning, making decisions, and in the daily management of the organization. It provides reasonable assurance that performance will be optimized, objectives achieved, and desired levels of value delivered to stakeholders.

2: Risk management provides decision-makers with reliable, current, timely, and actionable information about the uncertainty that might affect the achievement of objectives.

3: Risk management is dynamic, iterative and responsive to change.

4: Risk management is systematic and structured.

5: Risk management is tailored to the needs of the organization and updated/upgraded as needed. This takes into account the culture of the organization, including how decisions are made, and the need to monitor the program itself and continually improve it.

6: Risk management takes human factors (that may present the possibility of failures to properly identify, analyze, evaluate or treat risks) into consideration and provides reasonable assurance they are overcome.

While we are changing the world, let's have another look at the definition of risk management, starting with the COSO definition.

"Enterprise risk management is a process, effected by an entity's board of directors, management and other personnel, applied in strategy setting and across the enterprise, designed to identify potential events that may affect the entity, and manage risk to be within its risk appetite, to provide reasonable assurance regarding the achievement of entity objectives".

Let's take this one phrase at a time, starting (at the end) with the purpose of risk management: the achievement of entity objectives.

I agree that should be the result, and I like the fact that it is present in the COSO definition.

I also agree that the management of risk does not provide absolute, only reasonable assurance that the organization's objectives will be achieved.

The central part of the COSO definition, and in many ways its essence, is that risk management manages risk to be within the organization's risk appetite. I think COSO would have done better to say that risk management provides reasonable assurance that risks are at acceptable levels. That picks up a number of important points:

- Risk management processes are not perfect, but they can provide a reasonable level of assurance that appropriate actions are being taken with respect to uncertainty. By that, I mean a level of assurance that a reasonable individual would believe sufficient, given the cost of the additional investment that would be required to improve the likelihood that risks are at acceptable levels. (Later, in chapter 17, we will talk about the risk that risk management is not effective.)

- It is neither necessary nor desirable to eliminate risk. Risk is essential if the organization is to create value. The key is to take the right risks, at desirable levels.

> *Key point*: Risk management processes are not perfect, but they can provide a reasonable level of assurance that appropriate actions are being taken with respect to uncertainty.

- Whether the level of risk is acceptable depends on its effect on the organization's objectives and the cost of modifying it. This is important when multiple individuals are making decisions and taking risks, and the aggregate effect of those decisions has to be measured against desired levels.

The definition says that risk management should identify potential events that may affect the entity. I could quibble (some have) that uncertainties are not necessarily 'events', but that doesn't worry me – we can accept it in the definition as long as we understand that 'events' can include situations and circumstances.

But, I do not agree that risk management should identity potential events that may affect the <u>entity</u>. We should be concerned about what might affect the achievement of the <u>objectives</u> of the entity.

That point highlights a failing of many risk management systems. They don't start with an understanding of the organization's objectives and then identify risks to their achievement. Instead, they start with something they are worried about (such as systems disruption) and then, perhaps, wonder what objectives might be affected. This bottoms-up process results in worrying about risks that may not be significant to the organization's objectives, only of concern to individual managers or functions within the organization. It may also result in overlooking risks that are significant but have not been identified by their bottoms-up process.

Continuing to follow the definition backwards, we find that risk management should be applied in strategy setting and across the organization. This is excellent! Many omit the significant role that the consideration of risk should play in the setting of strategy. If the strategy is wrong, achieving it is not going to lead to the best result for the organization. It is also excellent that the definition talks about being applied across the organization, rather than being limited to a separate, siloed operation.

But, what is missing from the definition is the key phrase, 'decision-making'. Risk management should be applied as an integral part of decision-making at every level across the organization.

The definition says that risk management is effected by the board, management, and other personnel. I like that it paints a broad picture, involving the entire organization's personnel – and even the extended enterprise, including contractors, strategic suppliers, channel partners, etc.

Finally, the COSO definition says that risk management is a process. Now I know that some object, saying that risk management is a process *and* a framework[46] (discussed later), including a mandate, policy, and more. However, I am accustomed to considering policies and procedures as part of the process, so this doesn't bother me. On the contrary, I like the fact that it emphasizes the fact that we should think of the management of risk as a sequence of steps: identify, analyze, evaluate, and treat if necessary. (I just wish the COSO ERM Framework was more clearly structured to explain and illustrate the process, rather than confuse us by talking about components.)

How would I change the definition? I think I would tinker with it so it looks like this:

> "The effective management of risk enables more informed decision-making, from the setting or modification of strategy to the decisions made every day across the extended enterprise. The processes and related policies, structures, and systems for identifying, analyzing, evaluating, and responding to risks are established by management with oversight by the governing body to ensure that the effects of uncertainty (both positive and negative) on the achievement of objectives are understood and managed consistent with the desires of the governing body, for the purpose of achieving objectives, acting with integrity, and delivering optimal value to the organization's stakeholders."

This is, frankly, too long. An argument could be made that we already have enough definitions. But, I think this brings out some key points:

1. The definition highlights the role of risk management in enabling informed decisions. Better decisions lead to better performance and a greater likelihood of achieving or surpassing objectives.

2. It captures the need for decisions made in the setting or modification of strategy to consider risk. If the wrong objectives and strategies are established, achieving them is not necessarily right for the organization and its stakeholders.

3. The decisions that are critical to success are made by personnel, at all levels; this is not limited to employees, but includes those who make decisions across the extended enterprise.

---

[46] This is the ISO 31000:2009 position.

4. Management is responsible for establishing how and why risk will be managed and the board or other governing authority provides oversight. (This is consistent with the COSO definition.)

5. Risk management includes not only addressing potential harms but also the seizing of opportunities to excel.

6. The right risks need to be taken, consistent with the broad direction and intent of the board.

7. The overall purpose of risk management is to help the organization succeed. This means delivering the most value possible for stakeholders, considering the need to remain compliant with both legal/regulatory requirements and the values of the organization (i.e., acting with integrity)[47]. Delivering optimal value requires taking advantage of opportunities and limiting the likelihood and extent of harm.

Summarizing, risk management should only be considered effective when it helps people make better decisions – decisions that consider the uncertainty between where they are and where they want to go – and, as a result, increase the likelihood of getting where you want to go. That is fully consistent with both COSO and ISO, but I think it is much simpler than what either set of guidance presents as a way to assess effectiveness.

But, is there only one level of effectiveness? Can it be somewhat effective, or is the only choice between ineffective and world-class. For that, I think we need to look at the concept of maturity.

---

[47] The 'acting with integrity' concept is lifted from the OCEG definition of GRC.

Chapter 3: Risk management maturity

Very few organizations have what I would call effective risk management systems – based on whether they deliver what their organizations need if they are to make better decisions across the extended enterprise, optimize outcomes, and enable the achievement of objectives and strategies.

It doesn't matter whether you look at the COSO, Deloitte, or Aon studies I referenced earlier. They all confirm what I just said. The vast majority of organizations fall short.

We can add to that list of studies a 2014 survey[48] of internal audit leaders by the Chartered Institute of Internal Auditors[49]. Only 5% assessed their risk management system as "fully established and effective". This is astonishing given the UK requirement for listed companies to establish and then assess the effectiveness of their risk management system.

Maturity Models

Risk management maturity models are an excellent way for organizations to see where they are, compare their current state to where they want and need to be if they are to derive full benefit and discuss the value and cost of further investment in risk management. The more 'mature' the risk management system, the more effective it will be in enabling better decisions and better outcomes for the organization. As I mentioned earlier, some view the implementation of risk management as taking time. Using the term 'mature' instead of labeling the current state of risk management as 'ineffective' is less discouraging for its leaders, who often have struggled to implement risk management without the support from and investment by senior management it merits.

I developed the maturity model below a few years ago. It is based (with permission) on one developed for a local government agency[50] in the state of Washington.

---

[48] *Governance and Risk Report 2014: Internal Audit's Perspective on the Management of Risk*
[49] The UK affiliate of the Institute of Internal Auditors
[50] The Chelan County Public Utility District

It is not until you get to Level Five, in my view, that the management of risk should be considered mature. However, many organizations (and risk officers) seem content to be at Level Four or even Three. In Level Three, there may be a risk management policy and the ways in which risk levels are rated (e.g., high, medium, or low) are standardized. A report is provided to senior management and the board that summarizes the top risks.

Key point: Risk management maturity models are an excellent way for organizations to see where they are, compare their current state to where they want to be, and discuss the benefit and cost of further investment in risk management.

When you look at the additional capabilities of Level Five to integrate risk into strategy-setting and identify, assess, and address risk on a continuing basis, rather than once every so often, you can see the additional value that is created – because the higher level of maturity enables better decisions every day, not just every so often.

Maturity Level	Description	Key Attributes
One	Ad hoc	The management of risk is undocumented; in a state of dynamic change; and, depends on individual heroics.
Two	Preliminary	Risk is defined in different ways and managed in silos. Process discipline is unlikely to be rigorous.

Maturity Level	Description	Key Attributes
Three	Defined	A common risk assessment/response framework is in place. An organization-wide view of risk is provided to executive leadership. Action plans are implemented in response to high priority risks.
Four	Integrated	Risk management activities are coordinated across business areas. Common risk management tools and processes are used where appropriate, with enterprise-wide risk monitoring, measurement and reporting. Alternative responses are analyzed with scenario planning. Process metrics in place.
Five	Optimized	Risk discussion is embedded in strategic planning, capital allocation and other processes, and in daily decision-making. Early warning system to notify board and management to risks above established thresholds.

Grant Purdy[51] has an interesting maturity model[52] that merits careful review[53].

---

[51] Grant is the former Global Manager of Risk Management at BHP Billiton, one of the authors of the Australian/New Zealand risk management standard and ISO 31000:2009.

[52] Published in 2014 and included here with permission.

[53] Grant also has a definition of risk management that is not that different from mine: "Managing risk is a way of understanding and dealing with the effect of uncertainty on the organization's objectives in the course of decision-making. The process for managing risk must enable risk to be detected and

Stage	Description	Key Attributes
One	Risk Specific	• There are different types of processes for different types of risk • Risk categorisation is largely consequence based • There may be attempts at some form of 'integrated' measurement • Risk is seen as loss, harm and detriment • RM is closely linked to insurance. The terms 'risks' and 'hazards' and 'threats' are used interchangeably
Two	Driven by Governance	• RM is motivated by reporting • High level risk assessment is stimulated by reporting requirements, normally once or twice a year only • RM measures vary according to types of risk • Risks are seen as events – mostly with negative consequences • There are inconsistent approaches for managing different types of risk

understood and then modified as necessary in the most efficient way possible. Logically, this means it must take into account the views and knowledge of interested people, consider options and be able to detect and respond to change because the real world is not static."

Stage	Description	Key Attributes
Three	Driven by Change	• RM is associated with the management of change • RM processes are separate but are invoked by decision making processes • RM is driven by performance-based standards • Risk is seen as effect of uncertainty on objectives • There is a uniform system for the analysis of most types of risk
Four	Integrated	• RM is implicit in all decision making • RM processes are integrated in all key organisational processes • RM is integral to the system of management • RM is culturally driven – through performance standards • Risk is seen as effect of uncertainty on objectives • Effective RM leads to resilience and agility

In Grant's model, Stage One is where different 'types of risk' (such as risks from a failure in IT, sometimes inaccurately called IT risks[54]; supply-chain risks; and so on) are handled by different people in different ways. This is similar to what I have in Level Two.

---

[54] As will be discussed later, there is no such thing as an "IT risk". The only risks are business risks – the effect on the organization's objectives.

Grant also points out that in immature risk management systems only the potential for uncertainty to create harm is considered. Many organizations have tapped the manager in charge of their insurance function (often called a risk manager even though they are only responsible for obtaining insurance and possibly managing incidents and losses) to run their enterprise risk management system. These individuals often have a hard time adjusting to risk management concepts such as those in ISO 31000:2009 and the COSO ERM Framework. They continue to think of harm, threats, vulnerabilities, and so on, instead of the potential effects of uncertainty and the role of risk management in effective decision-making.

In Stage Two, the organization is responding to pressure from regulators and perhaps the board. The focus of the program is on creating a list of risks that can be reviewed by management and the board. The review is, by necessity, occasional. I have seen companies using consultants to facilitate a meeting of the top executives that comes up with a list of top risks. The list may only have 20-30 items on it, considered by the management team as the risks most likely to derail the organization. A couple of companies told me that they do this every two years, but most have annual or quarterly risk meetings to review and update the list. The board or a committee of the board reviews the list once or twice a year.

I don't consider this true risk management. My good friend Jim DeLoach[55] calls the practice of reviewing a list of top risks "Enterprise *List* Management".

When an organization gets to Grant's Stage Three, it is starting to have a meaningful risk management system. Recognition is given to the view of risk in ISO 31000:2009, the effect of uncertainty on objectives, instead of risk being seen

> **Key point**: The review of a list of top risks is Enterprise *List* Management

as the result of an event that harms the organization. There is also a focus on change, which is where most risk is created and lives. As in my Level Three, there is a fair degree of common language and even process across

---

[55] A Managing Director with Protiviti, Jim has been a thought leader and advisor to organizations globally on risk management and governance for more than 20 years. He advised COSO when it updated its Internal Control Framework.

the organization, but risk is not yet embedded in organizational processes or in strategy-setting.

Grant's and my top levels are similar. Risk is seen as a critical element in decision-making, embedded or integrated into organizational processes, and a key ingredient in the organization's successful achievement of its objectives and strategies, and both the creation and protection of value to stakeholders.

Once an organization achieves the highest level of maturity, it is almost certainly contributing to the success of the organization, as reported by Ernest & Young and Aon.

Risk management is not just a check-the-box activity, performed so that management and the board can assert compliance with laws and regulations.

Risk management is an integral part of how the organization is managed and directed, not just periodically but every minute of every day.

Organizations that have risk management systems at the highest level of maturity are likely to be answering Deloitte's question about contributing to the successful execution of strategies with a resounding "YES!"

> **Key point**: Risk management should be an integral part of how the organization is managed and directed, not just periodically but every minute of the day.

That is the true test of world-class risk management. The standards, frameworks, and maturity models may spell out the characteristics of world-class systems, but the only true test is whether the desired results are being obtained: world-class decisions.

What are so few at this level? Do the regulations and codes that organizations are expected to follow help or hurt? Why do so few understand the value of risk management when it becomes ingrained in how decisions are made, rather than set up as something separate or a check on decision-making?

Chapter 4: The current state of risk management and regulation

For the last several years, I have been talking to a large number of organizations about their risk management practices.

There is clearly a significant difference between organizations in different sectors and different geographies.

Most of the larger companies in financial services (especially banks, insurance companies, and similar) are not only used to managing financial-related risks in their portfolios, but are required by regulators to have risk management. Public companies that are listed on national exchanges in many parts of the world are required by local governance codes and regulations to comment on the effectiveness of their risk management systems in their annual filings.

In contrast, U.S. organizations in sectors such as manufacturing, retail, technology, and so on are not required either to have or to disclose publicly (except in a limited fashion[56]) how they manage risk and uncertainty.

Yet, even organizations where risk management is mandated do not always do it effectively. No, even the large global banks and other financial services organizations continue to be in the news for risk management failures[57] [58].

---

[56] There is a requirement to disclose 'risk factors', which should be the highest rated risks facing the organization, explain who is responsible for risk oversight, and say a few words about executive compensation risks (the risk that executive compensation might lead the CEO or other to; executives to put their interests ahead of those of the organization).

[57] According to a 2013 Bloomberg report, "The Financial Services Authority, which was replaced in April by the Financial Conduct Authority, levied 292 million pounds ($458 million) in fines against firms that didn't have adequate risk management and controls in place in 2012, up from 38 million pounds in 2011".

[58] A Wall Street Journal article in April, 2014, said that "Six years after the financial crisis, regulators remain concerned that banks lack insight into their own operations, including measuring risk and planning for a crisis.

Fueling those worries is that so far most large banks have failed to meet new heightened expectations on risk management outlined by the Office of the Comptroller of the Currency after the financial crisis. OCC officials, in an

A few years ago, I attended a presentation by a manager in one of the large accounting and consulting firm's ERM practice. She told us that risk management is all about calculating the level of risk, calculating the potential reward, and if the reward number is higher and the risk is within the organization's defined risk appetite, they should take the risk. It sounded just like gambling to me, not risk management. Her message was that risk management is about making sure that a trade was more likely to win than lose, and any loss would be within the organization's tolerance for losses.

She also explained that every risk could be modeled and a value calculated. I have run into this idea that every risk can be quantified several times with risk practitioners in financial services. Unfortunately, even if they are right and the risk is calculated to be "27", how does that translate in business language into something that will enable a business manager to take the right risk?

Deloitte has published a number of reports on risk management in the financial services sector, including the eight edition of *Global risk management survey* in 2012. I admit freely that I expected to see a large percentage of banks and other financial services companies identified as having upgraded their risk management systems from a limited focus on risk to their assets and portfolios to a broader enterprise risk management system covering all forms of risk to the achievement of objectives. I was wrong.

According to Deloitte, progress is being made. 89% of the institutions surveyed now have a chief risk officer, and 90% of them report directly to the CEO, meet with the board or risk committee, and participate in strategy discussions.

But, there are some significant signs of trouble.

Just 62% have an enterprise risk management system, with another 21% in the process of implementing one. They see risk as something bad that can happen to your portfolio, not something that is created or modified with every decision across the extended enterprise.

Fortunately, recognition that risk is more than what banks have traditionally addressed is growing – but it's clearly slow.

interview, said just two of the 19 firms subject to the new expectations meet the broad standards."

For example, only 80% of boards review and approve the institution's risk management policy, framework, and risk appetite statement (or equivalent). This is such a basic step for a bank or other financial services organization that I am stunned.

Reading the Deloitte report further, it says that "72 percent of the institutions rated themselves as extremely or very effective at managing risk". But, it is clear the respondents are only thinking of traditional financial risks. They rated themselves as extremely or very effective in managing liquidity risk (85 percent), credit risk (83 percent), counterparty risk (83 percent), and market risk (72 percent)". When asked about other areas of risk, the level of confidence dropped dramatically: "business continuity/IT security risk (52 percent), model risk (50 percent), and data integrity risk (50 percent)" with vendor/service provider risk at 45%, operational risk also at 45%, and human resources risk at 38%.

The regulators are slowly moving the bar, but when risk management is implemented in response to regulation it becomes a cost of doing business instead of a way to do business more effectively.

The regulatory guidance I have seen[59] is sound, but it is limited as it focuses on managing downside risks to the organization. Valuable elements of the guidance include:

- The board is held responsible for ensuring that the organization has effective risk management.

- The CEO and the executive team are directly responsible for managing risk.

- The board is expected to approve management's determination of the level of risk that the organization is willing to accept in the pursuit of objectives. (The regulators most often couch these levels using the term 'risk appetite'.)

---

[59] The most recent guidance is from the Bank for International Settlements (BIS) in their (draft, October 2014) *Guidelines: Corporate governance principles for banks* and the UK's Financial Reporting Council (September 2014) *Guidance on Risk Management, Internal Control and Related Financial and Business Reporting* (the latter apply to all listed UK corporations; the former is only for banks but is global).

- While quantitative models are accepted, they should not replace judgment and qualitative assessments of whether risk is acceptable[60].

- The risk management system should extend to routine decision-making across the organization.

- Attention must be paid to the risk culture of the organization, to ensure that risks are taken consistent with defined and approved risk appetite (or criteria). The topic of risk culture is discussed later.

Real and noticeable progress will be made when financial institutions embrace the last two bullets.

The regulators are understandably focused on the potential for a *negative* effect on the organization – understandable because they are concerned with management taking too much risk, putting the assets of the enterprise and the interests of the stakeholders in jeopardy.

They are much less concerned with organizations taking too little or the wrong type of risk.

A serious issue is that (as noted above) financial services organizations, encouraged by the regulators, have executives charged with risk management (typically with the title of Chief Risk Officer or CRO) that are independent of management. The concept is that an independent CRO serves as a check on 'cowboy' management, who are seen as quick to take high levels of risks because of the potential for reward. The result, however, is that the risk officers are seen as responsible for ensuring that the right risks are taken, rather than operating management. In fact, there can be significant tension between the 'cowboys' in management and the 'police' in risk management.

For example, a risk officer I know told me that traders would come to him with a proposed position. He would calculate the risk level (using sophisticated models and other techniques) and compare it to approved risk levels. But, the risk officer told me that if the trade was outside approved levels, standard practice (at his bank and elsewhere) was for the risk officer to deny the trade. The trader would argue, scream, and curse. He would go away and try something different[61].

---

[60] From the BIS draft guidance

This is not teamwork. This is not the risk expert and the trader working as colleagues to develop trades that are in the best interests of the company.

Instead, this is a model for the trader trying to make a trade that helps him achieve his bonus, and the risk officer putting on the brakes when the risks involved are calculated to be outside approved levels.

Only when both management and the risk officers work effectively together to consider options and take the right risk will performance be optimized.

The consulting firm of A.T. Kearney captured this in *Seven Tenets of Risk Management in the Banking Industry*. They said: "A.T. Kearney believes that the framework for risk management in a bank is fundamentally no different today than it was prior to the credit crunch and recession. Indeed, the risk function lacks a certain business acumen, and continues to be considered a handbrake on growth."

****

The other problem I have is the use of 'risk appetite'. I will discuss this in detail in chapter 13, but there is an important point I want to make first.

The guidance[62] typically asks management to propose and the board to approve the organization's risk appetite, which is generally expressed in

---

[61] My friend said he was the only one in his team that would try to work with the trader on alternatives. He would endeavor to restructure the trade or make other suggestions so that the trader could accomplish his objective and be within approved risk limits.

[62] The Financial Stability Board (FSB) published *Principles for An Effective Risk Appetite Framework* in November 2013. It advises financial institutions to establish a risk appetite framework that is "aligned with the business plan, strategy development, capital planning and compensation schemes of the financial institution." It sets "boundaries within which management is expected to operate when pursuing the institution's business strategy", but does not appear to recognize that risk is taken or modified with every decision. While the guidance recognizes the need to take sufficient risk and seize opportunities, it seems to be focused on a list of risks rather than helping decision-makers take the right risks every day, in every aspect of the business.

terms of a value. Then the risk management processes are focused on ensuring that this level is not exceeded.

However, as I have explained, risk management is about achieving or surpassing objectives.

I would prefer that organizations understand what might affect the successful achievement of each of their key objectives, both the situations that might represent a threat to their achievement and the opportunities to benefit.

Risk management should start with objectives and the risks to their achievement, then proceed to manage those risks to optimize outcomes. They should not start with risk appetite and then ensure that level is not exceeded.

From my understanding of risk management at the financial services organizations where I have either talked to risk officers or read about their practices, many fail to identify and then manage all significant risks to objectives. They are focused on threats to their investments and portfolio, rather than risks to their objectives.

But, at least financial services organizations have a formal risk management function that is recognized as essential and where the CRO has access to the top executives and the board. It may be seen as a policing function rather than contributing to optimizing outcomes in a more positive way, but it is involved in daily decisions that can create or modify risks to the success of the organization.

It is when you look at non-financial organizations that you see a disturbing level of immature and ineffective risk management.

I previously cited reports from Deloitte, Aon, and the Chartered Institute of Internal Auditors that told us that the current state of risk management was poor. This has been identified as an issue for organizations for a long time and it is refreshing to read reports that 80% of organizations are finally making investments in risk management – in people and, sometimes, technology.

But, my experience is that if they have a risk management function (beyond one that focuses on insurance and managing losses and other incidents), all it does is compile a list of top risks quarterly (sometimes annually or bi-annually) for management and the board. This is Grant's Stage Two and my Level Three maturity.

I have a passion and love for internal audit, and am proud to see so many internal audit leaders (chief audit executives, or CAEs) taking a leadership role and helping their organizations implement risk management. But, they frequently are doing so in their spare time (as if they have any) and with neither the resources nor the management mandate to strive for a fully mature risk management system.

Obstacles to Effective Risk Management

I believe there are a number of reasons for organizations not only having immature and ineffective risk management systems but being satisfied with them (see also chapter 18 on Assessing Risk Management Risk).

1. Management and the board simply don't understand the relationship between effective risk management and excellence in performance and delivery of value.

2. When there is a CRO, he or she is unable to explain the value of risk management. He or she talks in the language of risk and not in the language of the business.

3. There is little or no pressure from regulators to have quality risk management systems.

4. The CRO is satisfied with periodic assessments of a limited number of risks.

5. Consultants engaged by the organization promote the periodic assessment and review of a limited number of risks. These consultants often provide consulting services where they facilitate a quarterly (at best) discussion of risk by management.

The truth to the first point is demonstrated every day by executives and board members who accept the current state of risk management. They see risk management as a compliance exercise, protecting value (at best) and not something that enables the creation of value.

The root cause lies in the second point: the CEO doesn't see the value of risk management because the person in charge of risk management doesn't talk the language of the business.

The A. T. Kearney report captured this when they told this story:

A risk manager is overheard at a recent intra-departmental meeting: "The Basel II second pillar requires that we focus on the ICAAP, and it is inherent that the board of the bank fulfill their obligations in this respect and that sufficient oversight is provided by the SREP..." at which point many of the participants have no idea what the risk manager is talking about, but they are too afraid to ask questions so they nod their heads in polite agreement and hope no one will ask them for their personal opinion.

In *World-Class Internal Auditing: Tales from my Journey*, I tell a story of my own:

> I once gave a presentation at a risk management association conference. Afterwards, the president of the association asked to sit with me over lunch as he had a problem he thought I could help with.

> He told me that while he reported directly to the CEO, he always found it difficult to get time with him. When he was able to arrange a meeting, the CEO seem to lack interest in what he was saying and was reluctant to act on his recommendations.

> As this gentleman was speaking, I realized the problem. I didn't want to listen to him either, because he was boring! He spoke in a monotone without any passion in his voice, and used technical rather than business language.

> If I didn't want to listen to him over lunch, how could I expect a busy CEO to want to listen?

> When management doesn't find time to talk to you, or starts looking out the window as you are speaking, it's not a management problem. *You* are most likely the problem!

> We need to talk in the language of the business about things that matter to the business, and make sure the individual we are talking to understands how they affect him.

Effective risk management, let alone world-class risk management, requires that the CEO and the whole executive team embrace risk management as essential to their success. This won't happen if the CEO and executive team don't understand how risk management helps them be more successful, leading not only to corporate results but to larger bonuses.

A risk officer who talks about risk instead of performance, about protecting the organization instead of advancing it, about rules and regulations instead of revenues and profits, won't be persuasive – and in many cases that is because the risk officer himself doesn't understand how risk management (quoting Ernst & Young) gives management the confidence to *take* risk.

That is often the root cause of ineffective risk management: the risk officer is obsessed with *managing* risk, and doesn't see himself as helping the organization make better decisions, take the right risks, and optimize performance and outcomes.

> **Key point**: Effective risk management, let alone world-class risk management, requires that the CEO and the whole executive team embrace risk management as essential to their success.

To quote A.T. Kearney again, the risk officer's actions, words, and behavior justify management considering him "a handbrake on growth". Instead of enabling better decisions and outcomes, the risk officer is seen as inhibiting them.

Laws and regulations, including governance codes established by different countries, have had an uneven impact.

In the U.S., listed companies are required to comment, in the financials they file with the SEC, on "the company's compensation policies and practices for all employees, not just executive officers, if the compensation policies and practices create risks that are reasonably likely to have a material adverse effect on the company", and on "the extent of the board's role in the risk oversight of the company"[63].

However, there is no requirement by the SEC for the board or management to comment on whether they have a risk management system that meets the needs of the organization. There isn't even a requirement to disclose whether they have a chief risk officer or a formal risk management policy.

Other countries have gone much further. For example, Singapore has *Risk Governance Guidance for Listed Boards*[64]. It says:

---

[63] SEC release, 12/16/2009

The risk management process is an integral part of good management practices and should be embedded into the organisation's core business activities. Examples of the application of the risk management process in daily routines include the strategy setting process, investment decisions, health and safety policies, project management and change management practices.

The Securities Commission of Malaysia included guidance for listed companies in its last update of the *Code on Corporate Governance*. It has these two paragraphs:

The board must understand the principal risks of all aspects of the company's business and recognise that business decisions involve the taking of appropriate risks. This is intended to achieve a proper balance between risks incurred and potential returns to shareholders. The board must therefore ensure that there are systems in place which effectively monitor and manage these risks.

The board should determine the company's level of risk tolerance and actively identify, assess and monitor key business risks to safeguard shareholders' investments and the company's assets. Internal controls are important for risk management and the board should be committed to articulating, implementing and reviewing the company's internal controls system. Periodic testing of the effectiveness and efficiency of the internal controls procedures and processes must be conducted to ensure that the system is viable and robust. The board should disclose in the annual report the main features of the company's risk management framework and internal controls system.

As mentioned earlier, in the United Kingdom, the Financial Reporting Council (FRC) published an update of the UK *Corporate Governance Code* in 2014. Key points include:

30. The risk management and internal control systems should be embedded in the operations of the company and be capable of responding quickly to evolving business risks, whether they arise from factors within the company or from changes in the business environment. These systems should not be seen as a periodic

---

[64] Corporate Governance Council 2012

compliance exercise, but instead as an integral part of the company's day to day business processes.

31. The board should ensure that sound risk management and internal control systems are in place to identify the risks facing the company and to consider their likelihood and impact if they were to materialise.

57. Provision C.2.3 of the Code states that the board should report in the annual report and accounts on its review of the effectiveness of the company's risk management and internal control systems.

Unfortunately, as mentioned earlier, regulators tend to focus on preventing management and the board of an organization taking too much risk. They focus on protecting rather than enhancing value. This can be seen in the updated Code, when it says:

32. When determining the principal risks, the board should focus on those risks that, given the company's current position, could threaten the company's business model, future performance, solvency or liquidity, irrespective of how they are classified or from where they arise. The board should treat such risks as principal risks and establish clearly the extent to which they are to be managed or mitigated.

Hope remains that as the regulators upgrade rules and regulations to protect value they will, over time and with the influence of leading risk practitioners and institutes, start requiring organizations to disclose how their risk management systems contribute to performance. On the other hand, as Jim DeLoach pointed out to me, the regulators will probably have to be satisfied that organizations can manage threats effectively before they turn their attention to the creation of value for stakeholders.

* * * * * * * * * * *

Sometimes, the CRO not only doesn't talk the language of the business but doesn't understand the potential for risk management to enhance business performance.

A few years ago, I attended the annual conference of one of the main risk management professional associations. I remember a panel on ERM with four experienced practitioners. Each one of them discussed how they had been responsible for the insurance programs at their companies before being asked to lead a new enterprise risk management system.

They received a question from an individual in the audience who told us he was a new enterprise risk manager. What, he asked, should he do if the level of risk, based on a higher level of accidents, increased. The first panelist immediately started talking about increasing insurance coverage. Unfortunately, the other panelists agreed. None of them started asking questions about why the frequency and impact of accidents was increasing. Not one talked about addressing the root cause and whether measures could be taken to bring the risk back to acceptable limits. Having worked for a decade in a company with multiple oil refineries, with my office right in the middle and surrounded by units that could catch fire or even explode. I am very sensitive to the need to take employee safety seriously.

Insurance should be the last thing a risk manager thinks of, not the first!

****

The 2010 COSO report on ERM, *Current State of Enterprise Risk Oversight and Market Perceptions of COSO's ERM Framework*, includes a graphic of the current stage of ERM for those who responded to their survey. The top level of maturity is "Systematic, robust and repeatable process with regular reporting of aggregate top risk exposures to board".

I don't know why the authors (all academics, but the paper was approved by the COSO Board) made no mention of embedding the consideration of risk into strategy-setting, decision-making, and organizational processes. The highest level of maturity in the COSO report only ranks in my maturity model as Level Three, and Stage Two in Grant's.

It may not be fair criticism, but it seems indicative to me that even those who study risk management may not be aware of its full potential.

What about the consultants?

I will give full credit to several of the consulting firms for their thought leadership. I have previously quoted work by Deloitte and their *Risk-Intelligent* series of papers is excellent. I have also seen good work by several others, including Accenture, Ernst & Young, Protiviti, Broadleaf, and Causal Capital.

But, often the publications issued as thought leadership are, in my opinion, lacking.

For example, many focus on providing us with a list of top risks. That may be a useful checklist to make sure you haven't forgotten something, but risk is something that is very specific to each organization. What is a high risk to one company may be less so to another, even in the same sector.

I would prefer to see more guidance from these firms on how to improve decision-making, how to guide individual managers so they know what are the right risks to take consistent with their organization's risk appetite, and how to embed the consideration of risk into everyday business processes.

The cynical would say that the firms are publishing guidance so they can obtain consulting engagements. Certainly, many of them have been able to obtain repeat engagements where they facilitate management workshops that define, assess, and decide on the treatment of the organization's top risks.

When management of companies look for help to consulting firms, who then sell quarterly risk assessments, is it surprise that many companies have not moved beyond such an exercise?

****

Let me close this chapter with an excerpt from *A structured approach to Enterprise Risk Management and the requirements of ISO 31000*, a 2010 publication by AIRMIC, Alarm, and the Institute of Risk Management.

> Risk management is a process that is under-pinned by a set of principles. Also, it needs to be supported by a structure that is appropriate to the organisation and its external environment or context. A successful risk management initiative should be proportionate to the level of risk in the organisation (as related to the size, nature and complexity of the organisation), aligned with other corporate activities, comprehensive in its scope, embedded into

routine activities and dynamic by being responsive to changing circumstances.

Chapter 5: The value of periodic reporting

I have been free with my criticisms of those whose risk management is limited to (per Jim DeLoach) enterprise *list* management.

But, when I started the risk management system at Business Objects, I started with such a list – and that may be the best place to start for many organizations.

In fact, I believe some form of periodic reporting is not only advisable but *essential* for good governance.

While risks are created and modified by individual decisions, there are some risks that are more than momentary and relevant to a single decision or point in time[65]. They need to be addressed on a continuing basis.

The management of risk should be a constant activity across the enterprise, an integral part of daily management and decision-making. However, every so often it is necessary and appropriate for management and the board to (as John Fraser puts so well) 'take stock' of the current situation.

What information do boards and management need? I believe they need two different views.

> *Key point*: The management of risk should be a constant activity across the enterprise, an integral part of daily management and decision-making. However, every so often it is necessary and appropriate for management and the board to 'take stock' of the current situation.

- The first enables them to determine how well they are traveling the path to their objectives. It will answer the questions "is the risk to the achievement of

---

[65] For example, as you approach a traffic light that is changing color from green to yellow, you have to decide whether to slow down and stop or to continue through the intersection. Once you have passed through the intersection, you have not only left the intersection behind but the risks relevant to your decision as well (unless you are about to be fined for running a red light).

each of our critical objectives at desired levels?" and "do we need to take action, such as changing plans and strategies?"

- The second will let them assess whether specific areas of concern, such as access to confidential information, are being managed appropriately.

Unfortunately, most executive teams and boards only receive the second – a list of so-called top risks. The report is typically built from the risk register that the risk officer maintains.

Heat Maps

Some prefer a heat map to illustrate the comparative levels (typically using a combination of potential impact and likelihood) of each risk. An example is shown below (five risks are identified by circles).

A heat map is very effective in communicating which risks rate highest when you consider their potential impact and the likelihood of that impact. The reader is naturally drawn to the top right quadrant (high significance and high likelihood), while items in other quadrants receive less attention. In the example below[66], the user of the heat map is encouraged to focus on the top right by bands that are drawn across the heat map: green for low risk, yellow for medium, and red for high risks.

---

[66] Shown here as an example of what others use, not one I would use myself for the reasons given.

Heat Map

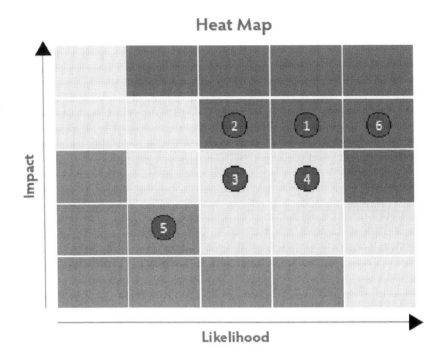

Likelihood

But there are a number of problems with a report like this, whether it is in the form of a heat map or a table.

1. It is a point-in-time report.

When management and the board rely on the review of a report that purports to show the top risks to the organization and their condition, unless they are reviewing a dynamically changing report (such as a dashboard on a tablet) they are reviewing information that is out-of-date. Its value will depend on the extent that risks have emerged or changed.

In some cases, that information is still useful. It provides management with a sense of the top risks and their condition, but they need to recognize that it may be out of date by the time they receive it.

2. It is not a complete picture.

This is a list of a select number of risks. It cannot ever be a list of <u>all</u> the risks, because as discussed earlier risks are created or modified with every decision. At best, it is a list of those risks that are determined to be of a continuing nature and merit continuing attention. At worst, it is a list of the few risks that management has decided to review on a periodic basis without any systematic process behind it to ensure new risks are added promptly and those that no longer merit attention are removed. In other words, the worst case is enterprise *list* management.

There is a serious risk (pun intended) that management and the board will be lulled into believing that because they are paying regular attention to a list of top risks that they are managing risk and uncertainty across the organization – while nothing could be further from the truth.

3. It doesn't always identify the risks that need attention.

Whether you prefer the COSO or ISO guidance, risks require special attention *when they are outside acceptable levels* (risk appetite for COSO and risk criteria for ISO). Just because a risk rates 'high' because the likelihood of a significant impact is assessed as high doesn't mean that action is required by senior management or that significant attention should be paid by the board. They may just be risks that are 'inherent' in the organization and its business model, or risks that the organization has chosen to take to satisfy its objectives and to create value for its stakeholders and shareholders.

This report does not distinguish risks that the organization has previously decided to accept from those that exceed acceptable levels. Chapter 13 on risk evaluation discusses how I would assess whether a risk is within acceptable levels or not.

4. The assessment of impact and likelihood may not be reliable.

I discuss this further in chapter 12 on risk analysis.

5. It only shows impact and likelihood

As I will explain in chapter 13 on risk evaluation, sometimes there are other attributes of a risk that need to considered when determining whether a risk at acceptable levels. Some have upgraded the simple heat map I show above to include trends (whether the level of risk is increasing or decreasing) and other information. But it is next to impossible to include every relevant attribute in a heat map.

6. It doesn't show whether objectives are in jeopardy.

As I mentioned above, management and the board need to know not only which specific risks merit attention, but whether they are on track to achieve their objectives.

On the other hand, some risk sources[67] (such as the penetration of our computer network, referred to as cyber risk) can have multiple effects (such as business disruption, legal liability, and the loss of intellectual property) and affect *multiple* objectives (such as those concerned with compliance with privacy regulations, maintaining or enhancing reputation with customers, and revenue growth). It is very important to produce and review a report that highlights when the *total* effect of a risk source, considering all affected objectives, is beyond acceptable levels. While it may not significantly affect a single objective, the aggregated effect on the organization may merit the attention of the executive leadership and the board.

---

[67] As noted in the Language of Risk section, many refer to these as "risks" when, from an ISO perspective, they should be called "risk sources" (element which alone or in combination has the intrinsic potential to give rise to risk). For example, the World Economic Forum publishes annual reports on top global risks, which it defines as "an uncertain event or condition that, if it occurs, can cause significant negative impact for several countries or industries within the next 10 years."

Risks to Objectives

While the executives and the board need information about individual risks (the second form of report), especially when they affect multiple objectives at an unacceptable level, the first form of reporting is *crucial* if risk management is to be seen as delivering essential value to the organization, its management, and its board of directors. The IFAC thought paper says (the key portion is highlighted):

> As risk is the effect of uncertainty on achieving objectives, it would be inadvisable to manage risk without taking into account the effect on objectives. Unfortunately, in some organizations **the linkage between the risks periodically reported to the board and the strategic objectives that are most critical to the long-term success of the company is at best opaque and at worst, missing completely**. As a consequence, risk is insufficiently understood or controlled, even though the organization devotes some attention and resources to the management of risk. Risk management without taking into account the effects on objectives is thus ineffective.

Both ISO and COSO talk about risk within the context of achieving (or, in my opinion, surpassing) objectives. ISO 31000:2009 defines risk as the effect of uncertainty on objectives.

Let's say that our company has defined an enterprise objective as "grow revenue by 10%".

A number of things have to go right and a number of things could go wrong, plus there will be opportunities to exceed the 10% growth objective.

Situations that might affect the achievement of "grow revenue by 10%" could include:

- The loss of key sales personnel affecting relationships with key customers
- A change (positive or negative) in the company's reputation for quality products that meet the needs of our customers
- A change (positive or negative) in demand from our customers
- A compliance issue that affects our ability to sell products

- A change (positive or negative effect) in the level of competition for our products

- Our ability (or lack thereof) to effectively market our products

- An improvement or degradation in customer support

- An improvement or degradation in our supply-chain

- An improvement or degradation in the quality and performance of our sales channel partners

- and so on………………

Each of these might be considered a risk itself, perhaps a 'risk source'[68]. But whatever you call them, these elements each have a likelihood and potential effect on the objective.

Management needs to know, at an enterprise level[69], whether the overall risk to the achievement of its revenue objective is at an acceptable level. That will require *aggregation* of the level of all of these risk sources.

It is possible that none of the risks above is at an alarming level. But, when they are aggregated the bigger picture could be of a large red flag.

Integrating Risk and Performance

The second report focuses on *risks*. The first report focuses on the achievement of *objectives*; it is much more *performance*-oriented and speaks to the desires of management and the board in their language.

Let me illustrate my point with an example.

A CFO is presenting the earnings forecast to the board. Included in that forecast is the revenue projection, and we have an organizational objective of "grow revenue by 10%". The forecast says we will meet that objective.

---

[68] ISO 31000:2009 defines a risk source as an "element which alone or in combination has the intrinsic potential to give rise to risk."

[69] Management at lower levels will own the management of the subordinate risks/risk sources, requiring aggregation to their level as well.

The chair of the audit committee asks the CFO how confident he is that the company will either achieve or exceed the revenue projection. Does the CFO answer by talking about all the individual risks and risk sources we listed? No. He gives his assessment of the likelihood of achieving or exceeding the revenue number by (a) considering actual revenue to date (a performance metric), and (b) his view of the overall (i.e., aggregated) risk to the objective.

So while it is useful when managing individual risks to review a list of risks, when you manage the business you need a larger lens that enables you to understand the overall level of risk to each objective.

When you understand the overall level of risk to an objective, you can recognize when there is a need for action. That may include action to modify one or more of the risk sources, or it might include changing strategy entirely.

In John Fraser's book[70], *Implementing Enterprise Risk Management*, Larry Warner[71] writes about the implementation of risk management at Mars, Inc. He includes a chart similar to what I have described. My adaptation[72] of his chart looks like this.

Business Objective	Risk Status
Grow revenue by 10% on a year-on-year basis	
Launch the new branded product by 6/30	
Improve customer satisfaction by 8%	

Rather than try to put a value for the level of risk, this report indicates whether the condition of risk[73] is acceptable (green), needing attention (yellow), or unacceptable (red).

---

[70] Co-edited by Betty Simkins and Kristina Narvaez

[71] President of Warner Risk Group

[72] Larry uses the term 'initiative', which I have changed to 'business objective'. Instead of his term, 'risk profile', I prefer 'risk status'.

[73] The assessment should be that of the risk owner. Where the owner of the business objective is different, the perspective of the risk owner should lead the assessment of risk status in the integrated dashboard, below.

I prefer a report that *integrates* risk and performance information. In many situations, the manager needs to know the current level of achievement (performance) as well as the current level of risk. In other words, the report shows both key performance information and key risk information.

In my presentations, I use the example of a manager whose objective is to drive from his office to his home. Looking at performance data (his metrics) he can see that he is halfway home and is traveling at 60 m.p.h. on the freeway. When he can see risk information as well as performance information, he can also see that the traffic 30 feet ahead has come to a total stop.

An example of a report that combines performance and risk information is shown below.

Business Objective	Risk Status	Performance Status
Grow revenue by 10% on a year-on-year basis		
Launch the new branded product by 6/30		
Improve customer satisfaction by 8%		

In my last year with SAP, one of the risk management leaders showed me an iPad app he was developing for the senior executive team. Each would be able to see, on a single screen, each of his or her objectives with an indicator as to whether everything was "green" (on target), "yellow" (potential issues), or "red" (serious issues). By clicking on the objective, the executive could drill down to the next level and see detailed information about its status. That information would include both performance and status information, presenting the information that the executive needed to understand and initiate appropriate actions.

This is risk information, integrated with performance information, that helps executives make decisions not only to manage risks but to optimize outcomes and achieve objectives.

Some risk practitioners have taken a middle ground in their reporting. They provide a list of risks, but they identify for each risk which objectives are affected. This is a significant improvement on a list of risks without context, but it falls short (in my opinion) of what management needs. It doesn't tell them whether they are likely (at an acceptable level) to achieve their critical objectives.

World-Class Risk Reporting

This is how I summarize the points above:

1. The review of a list of risks is likely to fail to connect with the focus of leadership on performance and value. Management and the board need to know whether the risks to the achievement of their objectives are at acceptable levels.

2. On the other hand, some risk sources affect multiple objectives; the executive and board leadership should receive information about those risk sources where the aggregated effect on the organization exceeds acceptable levels.

3. Any list of risks will be out-of-date because we live in a dynamic, fast-changing world. Reviewers need to understand and take this into account in their use of the list.

4. Any list of risks will always be incomplete because risks are created or modified with every decision.

5. Aggregation of risks is necessary to show the overall risk to any objective. This is a complex exercise that many fail to get right.

6. In order to make intelligent decisions, people need information about the status of performance as well as risk – integrated performance and risk information about specific objectives

Boards and management need to review risks to the achievement of objectives, together with performance data, on a regular basis. If they don't do this, how can they tell whether everything is heading in the right direction as intended? How can they tell whether they should continue with their current strategy, change direction, increase speed or slow down, or even stop?

They also need to see a report when the aggregated effect (on multiple objectives) of a risk source exceeds acceptable levels.

Bottom line: I believe executive management and the board should receive *two* reports:

- One that helps them understand if they are likely to achieve their objectives, a report with integrated risk and performance metrics, and

- One that highlights risks where the aggregated level is unacceptable

In addition to these two periodic reports, the board or committee of the board should receive a formal report, at least annually, from the internal audit team that provides an independent and objective assurance on the management of risk across the organization. That is discussed in the chapter on board oversight.

****

What should these reports look like? I have criticized heat maps but have not proposed an alternative – and I am not going to recommend a specific form now (although I do like the interactive dashboard that SAP developed for its executives, which is linked to strategies and objectives, has drill down and query capability, and is linked to the enterprise system so that it is constantly updated).

Rather than focusing on the form of a report, I believe we should focus on what information the users of that report need. Typically, they need the report so they can do one or more of the following:

- Obtain assurance that management has a reasonable understanding and appreciation of the risks to the organization's objectives, and is taking action as needed (CEO and board).

- Frame a discussion to confirm management's identification, assessment, and management of risk (executive management team, risk committee, and the board).

- Obtain information to drive action on risks to objectives for which the user is responsible (management at all levels).

The form of the report should be tailored to meet the needs of its users. That may mean that multiple forms are needed for different users, especially when different managers want the information in totally different ways. Some want only to be informed of risks that are outside acceptable levels and merit their attention, while others want to review a detailed list of risk. Some want to see everything on paper, others in a dashboard, and others want a briefing.

A world-class organization ensures that everybody who needs information about risk receives it in a way that is efficient and effective for them (with minimum compromises being made in the name of standardization).

But risk management is so much more than producing and reviewing a report, even a list of objectives and the risk to their achievement. Organizations cannot stop there; they have to make sure uncertainty and its effect, risk, are an integral part of strategy-setting and decision-making, and embedded in business processes across the extended enterprise.

Chapter 6: Embedding risk management into strategy-setting

There's not a lot of point in managing risks to your objectives if your objectives are wrong.

That would be like making sure the path to and over the cliff is clear. IFAC's thought paper says "Setting objectives itself can be one of the greatest sources of risk."

While both COSO[74] and ISO[75] talk about 'embedding risk into strategy-setting', they say very little[76] about making sure the organization has chosen its objectives[77], strategies, and plans wisely.

We live and work in a world that is characterized by what McKinsey has called "pervasive, ongoing uncertainty"[78]. Organizations thrive if they are able to take advantage of fair weather opportunities in our uncertain world while taking care not to founder on its reefs during a storm.

How can an organization set the right objectives, strategies, and plans if it doesn't have a reasonable understanding of the environment[79] into which it sails – when that environment is highly likely to be significantly different not only from this year but from any year it has ever experienced? What if the organization itself has changed, becoming more or less agile and able to maneuver at speed?

---

[74] "Enterprise risk management is a process, effected by an entity's board of directors, management and other personnel, applied in strategy setting and across the enterprise..." (From the COSO definition of risk management.)
[75] "In particular, risk management should be embedded into the policy development, business and strategic planning and review, and change management processes." (4.3.4 of the standard.)
[76] The section on Objective Setting says: "Enterprise risk management ensures that management has in place a process to set objectives and that the chosen objectives support and align with the entity's mission and are consistent with its risk appetite".
[77] I am not going to try to distinguish objectives and strategies. Some talk about strategies as how you achieve your objectives; others talk about objectives as how you measure whether you are achieving your strategies. I am going to use whichever expression makes more sense in what I writing.
[78] *Managing the Strategic Journey*, McKinsey Quarterly, July 2012
[79] ISO 31000:2009 refers to this as the external environment.

Will an organization sail in the right direction, in the best available vessel, if it doesn't understand how its world is changing (or is about to change) in one or more of these ways?

> *Key point*: Organizations thrive if they are able to take advantage of fair weather opportunities in our uncertain world while taking care not to founder on its reefs during a storm.

- The health of the economies in which it operates

- Its customers' needs and desires

- Competitor offerings

- The regulatory environment

- The introduction of disruptive technology

- The availability of the personnel needed to thrive (retention as well as hiring)

- The cost and/or availability of the services and materials needed to fuel the enterprise

What will happen in any of these dimensions is highly uncertain. Nobody has a crystal ball that guarantees the future into which we venture.

The best we can do is to take reasonable steps to understand what is most likely to surround us in the near and longer-term future.

My view of risk management is that it should help management and the board to understand the world in which they will operate; otherwise they may be setting an objective that is equivalent to setting the desired speed at which you will drive over the cliff or sail onto the reef.

In fact, I believe there are three ways in which we need to manage uncertainty:

1. We need to manage the possibility that our understanding of the environment is flawed.

2. We need to manage the possibility that, even if we understand our environment, we do not select the best objectives and strategies.

3. We need to manage risks to the achievement of those objectives and strategies.

> **Key point**: Risk management should help management and the board to understand the world in which they will operate; otherwise they may be setting an objective that is equivalent to setting the desired speed at which you will drive over the cliff or sail onto the reef.

This chapter is where I share my thoughts on the first two.

As I said earlier, people have been considering risk since the dawn of time. Risk management provides discipline so that the right risks are taken: when strategies and plans are established, and decisions are made.

People have similarly been looking at the world around them and making assumptions and projections about the near and longer-term future for centuries.

What they have not necessarily done well is recognize whether:

- They have an acceptable level of vision into the future

- Whether there is anything more they can and should do to improve that vision

- What might happen if they are wrong, and

- Whether they should be better prepared to handle the situation if they are in fact wrong.

One way to think about this is to identify, analyze, evaluate, and then treat as necessary the possibility that our vision of the near and longer-term future is wrong.

Understand the Assumptions behind Strategies

When management and the board start the process of setting strategies and objectives, they make a number of assumptions (including preconceptions) about the near and longer-term future. Those assumptions should be tested along the following lines:

1. What level of confidence do you have that the assumptions reflect the future? Is that an acceptable level of confidence? What

can and should you do to increase your confidence in the assumptions?

2. Have you considered *all* the ways in which the environment is going to change, how those changes may affect the organization, and how the organization needs to respond? This question, by itself, merits a workshop with the participation of a spectrum of functional and business unit executives so that sufficient time is given by all the people with relevant insights.

3. Do you have ways of monitoring change so that you can modify your strategies and objectives when appropriate?

4. Do you have agility within the organization so that it is capable of changing direction?

One aspect of risk management that I rarely see mentioned is that when the risk to objectives is beyond acceptable levels, one possible response is to change your objectives and strategies. Why continue to run into a brick wall between you and your desired destination (say, the beach)? Too often, the risk response involves adding speed or mass with which to hit the wall, when sometimes it is better to change the objective to an alternate destination (say, go to the zoo instead).

Once we have done all that we should to understand the environment in which we will operate, we need to make sure we set the 'right' objectives.

The Strategy-Setting Process

Deciding on the best strategy for the organization is not only critical; it is easy to get wrong – even when you have some of the best minds working on it.

Here are some thoughts on the strategy decision-making process.

- The estimated value created by each option is based on assumptions.

- The level of confidence in those assumptions must be understood and factored into the potential value. For example, is it better to be 90% confident that you can achieve at least $5m in sales from a new product in the first year or 80% confident that you can achieve at least $6m? (I discuss this question in the chapter on Risk Analysis).

- In addition to the stated assumptions, it is important to identify not only what could go wrong but what is needed to go right. Many assumptions are never actually stated; they are assumed (pun intended) – such as remaining in compliance with applicable laws and regulations.

- The potential impacts and their likelihood of those risks need to be understood and factored into the comparative assessments of each option. In fact, I prefer to see all forecasts and projections risk-adjusted. (I will leave the explanation of risk-adjusted forecasting to those with far more expertise than I[80].)

- Whether the potential impact and likelihood can and will be modified should be factored in, and the costs of doing so included in any cost estimate.

- The right people need to be included in the decision-making process. It is critical to obtain the insights of all who will be tasked with execution of the strategy (including functions like information security) and those whose knowledge will improve the quality of decision-making (such as the tax department, marketing compliance, government relations, and so on).

- The bias of key decision-makers must be considered. For example, it is easy to dismiss ideas, especially from people junior to you, if they are not consistent with your thinking.

- One of the problems facing some boards is that the CEO will often only present *his* preferred strategy; directors are unable to challenge him because they don't know what the options are. This is an issue the board needs to address by setting expectations with management.

- It is important to identify how management and the board will be able to monitor progress and evaluate the success of the strategy.

---

[80] For example, Deloitte published *Risk-Adjusted Forecasting and Planning* in 2012, and the Association for Financial Professionals published *Demystifying Risk-Adjusted Forecasting* in 2014.

Metrics should be identified and measures taken to capture them as part of the strategy-setting process.

One question I hear asked is whether the chief risk officer (CRO) needs to be a participant in the strategy-setting process. My view is that the effective consideration of uncertainty must be integral to the strategy-setting process – and that can be achieved with or without the CRO being present. Certainly, the CRO can be a mentor and facilitator as required. But, if management has been properly trained, then the CRO can be an on-call specialist. He doesn't have to be present for the full process.

Strategy-setting is, far too often, something that is done in secret. I worked at one company where the end-product was called the Sun Tzu document. An elite group worked on it and when it was completed it was kept in a vault, away from curious eyes.

This was a serious mistake. Operating management needs to know in which direction and towards what objectives management and the board want to sail the organization. If they don't know, who can blame them for taking actions that pull the vessel in a different direction? Who can blame them for failing to take advantage of opportunities to increase speed in the desired direction?

Who can blame them for taking the wrong or an unacceptable level of risk? They cannot identify, assess, and manage risk to objectives if they are not familiar with the organization's short and longer-term strategies and objectives.

In fact, many organizations fail to optimize performance because they don't ensure that all actions necessary to achieve objectives are included in individual and team performance metrics. But that's a topic for another discussion.

Chapter 7: Embedding risk management into daily decision-making and business processes

My friend Grant Purdy is one of the most respected names in the risk management profession. He was a leader in the development of the excellent Australia and New Zealand risk management standard AS/NZS 4360, as well as a major figure in the development of the ISO 31000:2009 global risk management standard.

So I was very pleasantly surprised when he told me that when he is engaged to help an organization upgrade its risk management, he doesn't meet with management to talk about how they manage risk. No, he asks them how they make decisions!

Over the last few years, Grant and I have had a number of discussions about whether risk management is something separate from the art of management. We both believe it is not: it is an *essential* skill for an effective manager. The ability to address uncertainty is fundamental and necessary. Unfortunately, it is infrequently included in the syllabus of MBA programs, let alone in in-house management training programs.

In fact, as I mentioned earlier, I believe that making risk management a distinct and separate 'profession', with its own standards and professional organizations, may even be harming its successful practice!

Two ISO 31000:2009 principles apply:

> 2: Risk management is an integral part of all organizational processes

> 3: Risk management is part of decision making

The ISO text for principle 2 is excellent:

> **Risk management is an integral part of all organizational processes**.

> Risk management is not a stand-alone activity that is separate from the main activities and processes of the organization. Risk management is part of the responsibilities of management and an integral part of all organizational processes, including strategic planning and all project and change management processes.

I want to emphasize that:

> *Risk management is not a stand-alone activity that is separate from the main activities and processes of the organization.*

When organizations establish a risk management function and talk about the Chief Risk Officer as responsible for the risk management system, there is a significant likelihood that operating management will see risk management as "not my job", "something required by the regulators (or other authority figure)", "something that gets in the way of my doing my job", "bureaucratic red tape", "a cost of doing business", or worse.

When boards look to the Chief Risk Officer (or worse, the head of internal audit) to assess and report on risk, they are absolving management from that responsibility.

When risk management is seen as 'something we do once a quarter', it is seen as an exercise separate from how the organization is managed every minute of every day. It is separate and not contributing to its success. At best, it is something that can help avoid disasters, similar to the periodic earthquake drills and contingency planning exercises (neither of which is really taken seriously by employees or management).

This is how the board, executives, and employees across the organization should see risk management.

> *Risk management is part of the responsibilities of management and an integral part of all organizational processes, including strategic planning and all project and change management processes.*

The text for principle 3 is correct but not as valuable as with principle 2:

> Risk management helps decision makers make informed choices, prioritize actions and distinguish among alternative courses of action.

Grant talks about decision-making rather than talking about risk management. I believe he does it for two reasons: (a) every decision creates or modifies risk[81]; and, (b) Grant is talking the language of the business, using terms that they understand. He is connecting with them and making it clear that he is talking about how they run their business; he is going to help them be more successful.

When I talk to a group about how we can effect change, I say that we need to understand this acronym:

WIIFM

"What's in it for me?"

A few people are motivated to act in the best interests of others, such as the company, their team, or their manager.

Most people are motivated by something that helps themselves.

We know that effective risk management will help them make better decisions and increase the likelihood and scale of their success. But most people don't think about risk management driving personal success. We need to help them make that connection.

If we can talk about more informed, quality decision-making, then everybody can see how that will help them personally and as a member of the organization.

We can appeal to their WIIFM, obtain their support, and with it effect change.

Grant helps them make better decisions and, through that, obtain both their support and effect change and improvement in the management of risk.

---

[81] Australia Standards HB 436:2013 says "The importance of applying the risk management process to decisions is because risk is generated or modified when decisions are made and acted on. However, decision-making occurs constantly throughout every organization – and ranges in significance from strategic decisions affecting the future direction of the organization to operational decisions through which daily tasks are completed."

Decision-Making

I do not profess to be an expert in the science called 'decision analysis[82]'. But there are a number of useful guides[83] on the basic process of decision-making. They describe the decision-making process as a number of steps. Although experts vary on the number and descriptions of the steps, they are generally as follows:

1. Define and understand the problem.

2. Gather all relevant information.

3. Identify and evaluate the options.

4. Select the preferred option.

5. Act and communicate the decision.

6. Follow-up as needed.

It is useful at this point to describe the basic risk management process (ISO 31000:2009 version[84]). After understanding the internal and external environments (i.e., our organization and the world in which it operates) and changes in those environments, risks are:

1. Identified

2. Analyzed

3. Evaluated, and

4. Treated

There is continuing communication, consultation with others, monitoring, and review.

As I look at the decision-making process and the 6 steps I listed, my first reaction – and probably yours – is that few people make decisions in such a systematic, disciplined way. Maybe we do this for the most important

---

[82] Decision analysis is defined by Wikipedia as "the discipline comprising the philosophy, theory, methodology, and professional practice necessary to address important decisions in a formal manner".

[83] They include *The Happy Manager: 7 steps in Decision Making"*, and UMass Dartmouth's model of the *Decision-making process*.

[84] Although COSO uses a slightly different structure, with components instead of process steps, it is essentially the same as the ISO process.

decisions and when we have the luxury of time. But, many of our decisions are made quickly and are based primarily on our experience: what worked last time is likely to work this time[85].

It's true that most of the bad decisions we make are made quickly. How often have we looked in hindsight at a poor decision and scolded ourselves for not taking the time to think about what we were doing?

So, the first thing worth recognizing is that slowing down and making more thoughtful decisions is a very good idea!

Let's consider the 6-step decision-making process one step at a time.

The first is to *"define and understand the problem"*. I think you have to combine this with the second step, *gather all relevant information*, because how can you understand the problem without all the necessary information[86]?

Many years ago, I was an IT audit manager and assessing the operating efficiency of my company's IT function. I saw some opportunities for improvement and told one of the IT executives about them. His reply set me back: "Norman, don't come up with answers until you really understand the question".

Because I hadn't done enough work to understand whether there was a problem, what the problem was at its root cause, and whether actions were already underway to address it, the brilliant insights I came up with weren't nearly as brilliant as I thought.

In fact, we often fail to take the time to obtain information and understand the problem before we make a decision.

Here's an example.

An HR executive is unable to hire the person he wants to fill an open slot as the recruiter for the IT department. He may assess the problem as one that impacts his performance evaluation, plus he will have the annoyance of having to deal with an upset CIO. But he's not thinking this through –

---

[85] See chapter 16 for a discussion of the human factors that can affect decision-making, such as bias.

[86] Some have a third step, *analyze the situation*, but I am including it in *define and understand the problem*. You can only define and understand the problem if you have the necessary information and analyze it.

and may not even have all the information necessary for him to realize the true nature of the problem. All he has seen is the surface of the problem.

In fact, the failure to hire a recruiter with specialized knowledge, experience and contacts means that open positions in IT are not being filled promptly. But the problem has more depth.

The failure to fill open IT positions means that several key information security and developer needs are not being met. Information security monitoring may be compromised and critical application development programs stalled or delayed. Now we are getting there.

These control weaknesses may affect the company's ability to protect confidential information, prevent business disruption, take advantage of enhanced technology, and meet important user needs for information required to set prices more effectively.

Adding the discipline of a risk management approach to the first two steps in decision-making should make it more effective.

For example, it is important to understand the context of the decision, in the same way that ISO 31000:2009[87] asks that we understand the internal and external context before we can identify risks.

- Why are we making this decision? What are we trying to achieve? Which business objectives are affected?

- If the decision is to address a problem, what are the potential (and perhaps actual) effects of the situation and how likely are they to occur?

- Who and what may be affected by the decision? Consider not only the current situation, but the situation after the decision.

The next step is to *identify and evaluate options*. What are the choices, which include deciding not to decide right now or deciding to take no action?

Risk management thinking is extremely valuable.

---

[87] Unfortunately, while ISO 31000:2009 establishes the principle "Risk management is part of decision making", neither the Standard nor the subsequent ISO technical report 31004:2013 *Guidance for the implementation of ISO 31000* provides anything that is helpful in understanding how this is achieved.

- If we decide to do nothing (or to defer a decision until later), we should consider what might happen. What would be the consequences of inaction, how likely are they (each consequence may have a different likelihood) and what effect will they have on our objectives.

- If we decide to do something, we should take each option and ask the same questions: what are the potential effects (all of them) and the likelihood of each?

- What actions can we take to optimize outcomes under each option (including when we decide not to act)? Can we reduce harmful effects, increase positive effects, and/or change the likelihood of each? Are the actions justified in light of their cost and benefits?

- As noted in the upcoming chapter on risk evaluation, are any of these potential effects outside acceptable ranges?

The decision-maker is frequently not in a position to answer all of these questions himself, because the decision he makes is likely to affect others – and he needs their input before he can assess the nature and likelihood of any and all effects on organizational objectives. That doesn't mean I believe a formal risk workshop is needed; I believe the decision-maker should consider who else is affected by his decision and at least consult with them so he can see the bigger picture before making his decision.

Select the preferred option and *Act, including communicating the decision,* come next. The risk management step of evaluating risk comes in here, where the potential outcomes of each option are evaluated – not only against each other, but against criteria that management sets (with board approval in some cases). Risk criteria (which include but are not limited to what COSO refers to as risk appetite) guide decision-makers in understanding what risks they should or should not take. (See the chapter on risk evaluation.)

Communicating the decision is very important, as one person's decision may not only impact others but may have a ripple effect. Others need to know so they can consider the effect on their own operations and take actions where necessary. For example, if the HR executive decides that none of the candidates for IT recruiter are acceptable, the IT team needs to know. They may move quickly, for example, to supplement their teams with temporary employees; if the problem is seen as continuing, IT may decide to outsource security monitoring or the development of an application (i.e., change their strategy).

The last step is to *follow-up as needed*. The decision-maker monitors what happens after the decision is made and acted upon. He needs to see whether things are going as expected or if there are indications that his assumptions and calculations were wrong (i.e., that his risk analysis was inaccurate). This may require additional decisions (i.e., additional risk treatments). The risk management process has similar monitor and review steps.

Decisions that would benefit from risk management thinking and discipline are far more frequent than you might expect. Standards Australia and Standards New Zealand's HB 436:2013 says it well:

> The importance of applying the risk management process to decisions is because risk is generated or modified when decisions are made and acted on. However, decision-making occurs constantly throughout every organization – and ranges in significance from strategic decisions affecting the future direction of the organization to operational decisions through which daily tasks are completed.

Decisions are being made whenever somebody does something characterized by one of these words:

- Approve
- Review
- Evaluate
- Select
- Choose
- Determine
- Award
- Estimate
- Judge
- Vote

- ...and more

So decisions are made almost every minute of every day. They are made in business processes such as:

- Treasury
- Procurement
- Budgeting and forecasting
- Legal
- Accounting
- Capital expenditure approvals
- Project management
- Product engineering
- Logistics
- Manufacturing
- Credit
- Sales
- Marketing
- Quality
- Application development
- Information security
- ...and so on

Almost every business process includes decisions and those decisions create or modify risk. The management of those risks should be considered part of those business processes and not a separate activity.

But does every decision require the discipline afforded by a formal risk management process?

It seems common sense to say that the more important a decision is, the more time should be given, the more there should be consultation and collaboration, and the more disciplined the process should be.

But what makes a decision important?

It's the potential effect of the decision on the organization and its objectives – in other words, the level of risk that is created or modified by the decision.

Risk Beyond the Organization

Before I close this chapter, I want to talk about the *extended enterprise*. Few organizations operate these days without relying on service providers, partners, and so on. Organizations need to understand that risks may be created or modified by the decisions of their partners and others within the extended enterprise. They need to know whether the effect and likelihood of a failure to perform on the part of a channel partner, for example, has increased to the extent that it is unacceptable.

Some organizations send their partners in the extended enterprise questionnaires about their management of risk. While this may provide a limited sense of assurance, I am not persuaded that it satisfactorily addresses the risks that are created or modified by the decisions and actions of those partners.

My preference is that the organization should establish who *within the organization* owns the relationship with each partner in the extended enterprise. That individual is responsible, in partnership with other functional areas of the organization, for understanding, monitoring, and assessing the risks related to the partner – and ensuring appropriate controls are in place.

I saw this fail when I was with Maxtor[88], responsible for internal audit and the Sarbanes-Oxley compliance (SOX) program.

The company had outsourced about half of its applications to a third party service provider. The applications included financial systems as well as systems that supported manufacturing and the development of new products. In other words, systems that needed to be protected, not only for SOX compliance but to support general business operations and secure its confidential information and intellectual property.

---

[88] Maxtor was a $4bn hard drive manufacturer. It was later sold to Seagate.

The service provider had engaged an audit firm to assess and test its controls and security. Our SOX program relied on the auditors' report for assurance that the controls operated by the service provider, including information security, were functioning as desired.

However, the service provider didn't send us the report at the normal time. I asked the IT manager to follow up but heard nothing. After a week or so, I called him again and while he voiced a modicum of concern, he told me that he didn't own the relationship with the service provider. I asked him who was the owner and he said he would find out (not a good sign!)

Eventually, I was able to talk to the manager who confirmed that he was the owner of the relationship – but he said he had very little to do with them beyond negotiating the initial contract and its annual renewal. He had no concept of the risks that Maxtor would be exposed to should the service provider fail to perform; he only knew what was in the contract in terms of penalties. He reluctantly agreed to chase the service provider for the audit report.

When we finally received the auditors' report, it included several serious control and information security issues. While we were able to navigate our way past the SOX issues, the company had been exposed for a significant period of time to an unacceptable level of risk from business disruption and the theft of intellectual property and confidential information.

The individuals responsible for the effect on organizational objectives were not responsible for monitoring the risk; in fact, I doubt they even understood the risk.

These managers were not very effective managers of the risks for which they were responsible. They had no risk management training and, unfortunately, the company did not have a risk management function that would help bridge that gap – not by taking on the responsibility for the management of risk, but by providing managers across the enterprise with the training, tools, process, and support they need to do so.

Chapter 8: The role of the risk officer

By now, I hope it is clear that I believe:

- The management of risk is an essential activity for every manager and every manager should be a 'risk professional',

- Every manager should have the understanding of risk management necessary to make decisions and create/modify risk within acceptable levels,

- The risk officer does not own the management of risk, and

- The management of risk is owned by those who have responsibility for achieving objectives,

An interesting 2010 article in *American Banker*, entitled "Don't Bank Too Much on the Chief Risk Officer" had this to say:

> The most serious misconception is that the chief risk officer really is the chief risk officer. The CEO is ultimately the chief risk officer because enterprise risk management is a fundamental leadership responsibility that cannot be fully delegated to anyone else. As Warren Buffet said in his latest letter to Berkshire Hathaway shareholders: "I believe that a CEO must not delegate risk control. It's simply too important. ... If Berkshire ever gets in trouble, it will be my fault. It will not be because of misjudgments made by a risk committee or chief risk officer."

It went on to say:

> Handing off full responsibility for the bank's enterprise risk management is the wrong reason to have a CRO. The result is likely to be an expensive compliance bureaucracy that creates a false sense of security. The CRO becomes merely an actor in a diverting farce that presents the façade of risk management without the reality of risk management. As many banks discovered in the financial crisis, this farce can turn into a tragedy when the music stops.

IFAC concurs:

> As an organization's risk is inextricably connected to its objectives, the responsibility for managing risk cannot lie with anyone other than the person who is responsible for setting and achieving those objectives.

Line management needs to accept its responsibility and not delegate risk management and internal control to specialized staff departments. Placing responsibility within the line also implies that staff or support functions should not, or no longer, be the "owner" of risk management in organizations. However, these support functions nevertheless play a crucial role in supporting line management in the effective management of risk.

If the risk officer doesn't own or have overall responsibility for the management of risk, what does he do? Why should an organization have one?

The *American Banker* gives us a good start to answering that question:

The CRO helps the CEO and the board implement a credible, consistent risk management framework to govern the bank's risk-taking across all businesses; provides expert, unbiased advice on risk issues; and offers constructive ideas that use smarter risk management to unlock new business opportunities.

What is the "risk management framework" that the magazine is referring to (not to be confused with the COSO *Enterprise Risk Management-Integrated Framework*)? Some think of it as the risk management policy or standard, but it should be much more (although the policy is clearly important if not essential).

The *Plain English ISO 31000:2009 Risk Management Dictionary*[89] explains that:

A risk management framework is a set of components that support and sustain risk management throughout an organization. There are two types of components: foundations and organizational arrangements. *Foundations* include your risk management policy, objectives, mandate, and commitment. And *organizational arrangements* include the plans, relationships, accountabilities,

---

[89] A more understandable description than the ISO 31000:2009 definition as "set of components that provide the foundations and organizational arrangements for designing, implementing, monitoring, reviewing and continually improving risk management throughout the organization

resources, processes, and activities you use to manage your organization's risk.

Although the *Dictionary* puts the risk management policy first in its list, effective risk management is totally dependent on support from the board and CEO.

I am talking about more than a mandate. Anybody can say "I believe in and support risk management", but if an organization is to live and breathe risk management, the CEO has to demonstrate his commitment to the management of risk – every day in every way.

It's not enough to have the CEO participate in risk management workshops and periodic reviews.

I want my CEO to require all of his direct reports to use risk management thinking in their decision-making, and to demonstrate that when they make presentations and proposals to him.

I want my CEO to not only *embrace* but to *embody* risk management thinking.

The management team has to believe that the CEO expects *them* to embrace risk management, as he does himself. I believe that when they do that, they will see how it helps them make better decisions that lead to optimized outcomes for them personally (appealing to their WIIFM) and for the organization as a whole. Once the executive team learns how to employ risk management thinking, they will demand it of their teams and the belief will spread.

> **Key Point:** I want my CEO to not only *embrace* but to *embody* risk management thinking.

The CRO is the risk management guide, the evangelist. The CRO 'spreads the good word' about the benefits of risk management, educates, explains, and provides continued training and mentoring.

Many organizations will benefit from having the mandate and commitment confirmed and communicated in a formal risk management policy, preferably signed by the CEO and updated on a regular basis. Two examples, from BHP Billiton and CQ University Australia, are included in Appendices A and B respectively.

The risk management policy should be owned by the CRO, who should work in collaboration with senior management to ensure it spreads the word and includes or references all the formal guidance necessary. For example, the risk management policy at SAP "governs how we handle risk in line with the Company's risk appetite and defines a methodology that is applied uniformly across all parts of the Group. The policy stipulates who is responsible for conducting risk management activities and defines reporting and monitoring structures[90]".

An effective risk management system establishes a common language and more across the enterprise – such as how likelihood, impact, and risk levels will be described. It's the only way to form an enterprise-wide view of risk to the organization's objectives, to have a cross-functional workshop, or to discuss how the actions and decisions of one may affect another.

The CRO is responsible for this part of the risk management framework: the risk management policy, the common language of risk, and so on.

An excellent example can, again, be found at SAP. Their risk management policy stipulates that their risk management system is based on the COSO ERM Framework (and therefore uses the COSO risk terminology), establishes a common rating system for risks (likelihood, potential impact, and how the combination of the two determines the risk level[91]), and defines how different levels of risk will be reported. The policy explains and describes how SAP has assigned risk approval to different levels of management and the board. The company does this in the same way it assigns spending approval. In other words, lower level risks are reported to and overseen by lower levels of management than higher level risks.

The CRO has a number of other essential responsibilities:

- Providing enterprise-wide reports to executive management and the board (as discussed in the chapter on risk reporting)

- Arbitrating disagreements among managers on risk analyses, evaluations, and treatment

---

[90] The *SAP Integrated Report 2013*, from which this quote is excerpted, provides a wealth of detail on SAP's risk management system.

[91] SAP has a 5-level scale for likelihood, 5 levels for impact, and 3 risk levels: high, medium, or low.

- Facilitating cross-functional risk assessments and workshops

- Providing risk management training for new managers and decision-makers

- Providing subject matter expert assistance and mentoring as needed

- Monitoring and reviewing the risk management system to ensure it remains effective in meeting the organization's needs. This may include leading projects to upgrade the risk management system, such as the implementation of automated systems for risk monitoring and more

- Acting as the 'policeman' when management fails in its management of risk, especially when the CRO has a serious disagreement with the assessment and treatment of significant risks

There is always some level of turnover among an organization's executives, managers, and other decision-makers. New employees need to understand the organization's approach towards risk management, how the system works, and what is expected of them. I believe the CRO should either be delivering much of that training or ensuring that appropriate training is delivered.

Any organization's risks are changing almost every minute of every day as it makes decisions and as changes happen to the world in which it operates. It is impossible for a risk management team to ensure only the right risks are taken. Reliance has to be placed on individual managers and decision-makers.

There is an old saying, attributed to Maimonides: "Give a man a fish and you feed him for a day; teach a man to fish and you feed him for a lifetime". The same principle applies with risk management. If the management of risk is not owned by management but assigned to a risk management function (or worse, to internal audit), management will never learn how to analyze, evaluate, and treat risk. The likelihood that management will make poor decisions and take the wrong risks will be unacceptably high.

If an organization is to have effective, let alone world-class risk management, the CRO and his team must be enablers, teachers, and mentors to the true managers of risk: managers and decision-makers across the organization.

In a world-class organization, the management of risk is world-class: it is practiced even when the risk officer is not present.

In a world-class organization, the risk officer doesn't have to insert himself into management's processes for identifying, analyzing, evaluating, and responding to risk. Management asks for his help if and when they need it.

> **Key point**: In an ideal world, the management of risk is world-class: it is practiced even when the risk officer is not present.

In a world-class organization, the risk officer is welcomed to the table. His advice is sought when new initiatives are considered or problems encountered, and his students all graduate.

Few organizations today have achieved this level of effectiveness; it should be their goal. It is difficult to imagine that an organization can consistently achieve world-class performance, optimizing long-term value for its stakeholders, without world-class risk management.

Should the risk officer have a permanent seat at the table? Is it necessary for him to be independent and a direct report to the CEO with free access to the board? As noted above, the risk is that this will lead to risk being delegated to the CRO and his being the policeman instead of the mentor and subject-matter expert.

North Carolina State University has an Enterprise Risk Management Initiative led by Professor Mark Beasley[92]. In 2013, they published *Strengthening the Role of the Chief Risk Officer in an Organization*. Six issues were identified as crucial to the success of the CRO; I agree with their third point but am unsure about the others in a mature environment.

1. **Viewed as a Peer with Business Line Leaders** – In order to achieve the forward-looking risk perspective and its serious consideration, the CRO must be able to deliver those expectations through a collaborative relationship with business line leaders. Hence, the CRO must be viewed as a peer. Not doing so would

---

[92] Mark was an advisor to the team that developed the COSO ERM Framework

hamper the ability for the CRO to function effectively and misplace the CRO's direct reporting capability.

2. **Board Reporting and Interactions** – While the CRO is not an owner of specific risks, he or she has the task of executing a strategic oversight of the entire risk management focus that mandates free access to the board for conveyance and reporting. Not providing such access would cause disconnect in communication and the loss of resolutions to various strategic problems.

3. **Managing Risks is Everyone's Job** – The board, senior management and other line managers must remove the misconception that the CRO is the only person responsible for risk. Risk has to be an enterprise-wide concern. Thus, raising awareness and owning risks within operations to establish a risk-aware culture is imperative to a successful implementation of a CRO's function.

4. **Risk is Equal to Opportunity Pursuit** – Risk management functions to preserve value as well as create value. The best interests of the organizations are kept while pursuing these strategies to improve the organization. Nevertheless, organizations must realize limits in engaging in value-creating activities against value preservations controls. The CRO attempts to strike this balance through decision making and risk appetite formulation. An imbalance may raise the level of risk for the less proportionate aspect and create a setback to the organizations.

5. **Broaden Focus Beyond Compliance** – It cannot be stressed more than the fact that the focus of the CRO should be on the enterprise risks, risk profile and aligning strategy based on risks. This goes beyond compliance risks and raises the bar for the CRO. While the CRO has to be in compliance with the laws and regulations, expanding the focus will make it easier for the CRO to have the desired impact in managing risks.

6. **Clearly Defined CRO Position** – Clearly defined CRO position should be in place in order to enhance the CRO's objectivity in fact and appearance. Setting the right expectation about the CRO's responsibility for promoting effective governance of significant risks is crucial in furthering the role of the CRO. Not

having clear definitions may cause the CRO to lose focus and extend resources in less important matters lowering the overall effectiveness of the CRO.

The importance of the depth and extent of the relationship the CRO has with senior executives and the board will enable the CRO to be in a stronger and more effective role to manage the overall risks instrumentally protecting the value that organizations have taken years to build.

The article tries to thread the needle between having management own risks and having the CRO in a leadership position. The logic doesn't work for me. I think it ends up placing more reliance than it should on the CRO taking strategic responsibility for risk, and not enough on the CRO being the teacher and guide to those in operating management who have responsibility for risk.

Frankly, I am not convinced that the CRO needs to be a direct report to the CEO in an organization that is fully committed to and practices risk management as an integral element of decision-making and running the business. If every executive and manager is a trained manager of risk, why do you need a high-powered risk management function[93]? Could somebody else provide executive management and the board with enterprise-wide reports? Yes – especially if the organization is able to integrate performance and risk reporting.

But, until the management of risk is part of the fabric of the organization, enshrined in its 'culture' (as will be discussed later), a CRO that has the position to be an effective evangelist, mentor and guide is essential. The CRO can help guide management in establishing the appropriate policies, standards, processes, and expectations for risk management; train managers and teams across the organization; and provide reports and work with the board so they can provide effective oversight.

---

[93] As Grant Purdy pointed out to me, there is always a chance that the presence of a CRO at a senior leadership meeting will lead people to believe that his presence alone means the consideration of risk was adequately considered in each decision.

The CRO as Policeman

Until the management of risk is mature, the CRO must be alert to weaknesses in its practice. Some managers, even senior executives, may be tempted to suppress bad news from reaching leadership or the board. The CRO needs to be very much aware not only that this might happen, but where – so he can monitor the situation and take action when appropriate.

There are times when the risk officer needs to act like a policeman.

Where the risk officer believes management is not participating in the program, even after he does his best to explain the value and that leadership expects active participation by every manager, he will have to escalate the situation to more senior management, even to the CEO and the board if necessary.

When the risk officer has a serious problem with the assessment of risk and/or the actions being taken by management in response (for example, accepting an excessively high level risk that could be mitigated or even avoided), he must bring that to the attention of senior management.

When reporting to the board, these are situations that the CRO should give strong consideration to sharing. The board needs to know whether it can rely on management to address risk to the achievement of objectives and whether the reports it is receiving can be trusted.

Chapter 9: Oversight by the board

There are a number of authoritative guides on the oversight of risk management by the board.

Risk management in Australia is, in many respects, ahead of most nations. The Australian Stock Exchange (ASX) published the third edition of their *Corporate Governance Principles and Recommendations* in March, 2014. Principle 7 is "Recognize and manage risk: A listed entity should establish a sound risk management framework and periodically review the effectiveness of that framework".

The Commentary to Principle 7 is useful. It describes why risk governance is important.

> Being given sufficient information to understand and assess investment risk is crucial to the ability of investors to make informed investment decisions. Recognising and managing risk is a crucial part of the role of the board and management.

> A failure by a listed entity to recognise or manage risk can adversely impact not only the entity and its security holders but also many other stakeholders, including employees, customers, suppliers, creditors, consumers, taxpayers and the broader community in which the entity operates.

> Good risk management practices can not only help to protect established value, they can assist in identifying and capitalising on opportunities to create value.

> The board of a listed entity is ultimately responsible for deciding the nature and extent of the risks it is prepared to take to meet its objectives.

> To enable the board to do this, the entity must have an appropriate framework to identify and manage risk on an ongoing basis. It is the role of management to design and implement that framework and to ensure that the entity operates within the risk appetite set by the board. It is the role of the board to set the risk appetite for the entity, to oversee its risk management framework and to satisfy itself that the framework is sound.

The last sentence sets the expectation for the board:

It is the role of the board to set the risk appetite for the entity, to oversee its risk management framework and to satisfy itself that the framework is sound.

That is fairly clear and succinct. It doesn't limit risk management to the protection of assets and value, but recognizes that risk management enables an organization to "identify and capitalise on opportunities to create value".

The document goes into more detail, but I prefer Singapore's *Code of Corporate Governance 2012*, which also has principles and guidelines. With respect to risk management, it says:

Principle:

11.   The Board is responsible for the governance of risk. The Board should ensure that Management maintains a sound system of risk management and internal controls to safeguard shareholders' interests and the company's assets, and should determine the nature and extent of the significant risks which the Board is willing to take in achieving its strategic objectives.

Guidelines:

11.1   The Board should determine the company's levels of risk tolerance and risk policies, and oversee Management in the design, implementation and monitoring of the risk management and internal control systems.

11.2   The Board should, at least annually, review the adequacy and effectiveness of the company's risk management and internal control systems, including financial, operational, compliance and information technology controls. Such review can be carried out internally or with the assistance of any competent third parties.

11.3   The Board should comment on the adequacy and effectiveness of the internal controls, including financial, operational, compliance and information technology controls, and risk management systems, in the company's Annual Report. The Board's commentary should include information needed by stakeholders to make an informed assessment of the company's internal control and risk management systems.

The Board should also comment in the company's Annual Report on whether it has received assurance from the CEO and the CFO:

a) that the financial records have been properly maintained and the financial statements give a true and fair view of the company's operations and finances; and

b) regarding the effectiveness of the company's risk management and internal control systems.

11.4 The Board may establish a separate board risk committee or otherwise assess appropriate means to assist it in carrying out its responsibility of overseeing the company's risk management framework and policies.

Both of these are far superior to most of the guidance I see in the United States, which typically focus on two issues: (a) having the board review and discuss a list of the top risks, and (b) whether the board has a sufficient understanding of risk management.

One U.S. publication stands out. This is the 2009 *Report of the NACD (National Association of Corporate Directors) Blue Ribbon Committee on Risk Governance: Balancing Risk and Reward*. The committee made ten recommendations:

1. Understand the company's key drivers of success.

2. Assess the risk in the company's strategy.

3. Define the role of the board and its standing committees with regard to risk oversight.

4. Consider whether the company's risk management system – including people and processes – is appropriate and has sufficient resources.

5. Work with management to understand and agree on the types (and format) of risk information the board requires.

6. Encourage a dynamic and constructive risk dialogue between management and the board, including a willingness to challenge assumptions.

7. Closely monitor the potential risks in the company's culture and its incentive structure.

8. Monitor critical alignments – of strategy, risk, controls, compliance, incentives, and people.

9. Consider emerging and interrelated risks. What's around the next corner?

10. Periodically assess the board's risk oversight processes: Do they enable the board to achieve its risk oversight objectives?

There is a lot of meat, rich in fiber and protein, in this diet of ten recommendations.

But there is one task I would have for the board that is not in any of these three documents.

Earlier, I discussed the need for the CEO to embrace and embody risk management thinking. I need the board to ensure this happens. The board should demand and expect the CEO, CFO, and other members of management to:

- Demonstrate that they are considering what might happen, analyzing it, evaluating it, and acting accordingly in the setting of strategy and objectives; planning, budgeting, and forecasting; the management of major initiatives; the daily operation and management of the organization; and, the measurement of performance

- Not only embrace and embody risk management themselves but set expectations for management and decision-makers across the organization to embrace and embody risk management thinking

- Make full use of the CRO as a subject matter expert

The board must have the mindset to challenge management to use a disciplined decision-making process that includes the consideration of risk before bringing anything to the board. Questions that might help include:

- What options have you considered?

- What assumptions have you made?

- What level of confidence do you have in them?

- What actions have you taken to improve their impact and likelihood?

- What is the range of potential outcomes, how have you risk-assessed them, and why have you selected this option?

- How will you monitor progress and changes in risk levels so that you know when to change direction or take other correct action?

Earlier, I talked about the fact that a review by the board of a periodic risk report is essential for risk oversight; I mentioned two reports: one that provided information on whether risks to the achievement of critical organizational objectives were at acceptable levels, and one that listed risks that individually merited board review (typically because they might affect multiple business objectives).

I also discussed the limitations of these reports, notably that they represent a point-in-time view that is already out of date by the time the board receives it and that it is certain to be incomplete – because risk is changing constantly. It has some value, but cannot be relied upon exclusively for assurance that the current level of risk is at an acceptable level.

The board needs assurance that management's attention to risk is continuous, not just when they are preparing for a presentation to the board.

Most of the modern corporate governance codes, such as the ASX and Singapore codes, as well as the NACD guidelines mandate that internal audit (usually) provide the board with a formal assessment of the risk management system at least once each year. The board can place a high level of reliance on this review, but should watch for indicators at every meeting that attention to risk is weakening – for example, when they are provided with a capital expenditure proposal without any discussion of risk.

The key remains, as it should, with the members of the board. Based on their interaction with management and the reports they receive from others, such as internal audit, do they have confidence in management's ability to address the uncertainty that lies between where they are now and where they need to be?

The Board's Risk Agenda

Should the board spend quality time discussing specific risks, as many consultants suggest?

I believe that's a matter for the board's judgment. I would ask whether they have confidence in management to address specific risks. If they do, what is the value of the board spending some of their limited time covering the topic?

Perhaps the members of the board can help management through a discussion of a critical issue, especially if they are able to challenge the CEO and his team and 'pressure test' their thinking. Probing management about their understanding and assessment of specific risks can help the board develop not only confidence in management's assessment of those risks, but in their ability to assess risks in general.

Perhaps individual directors have special knowledge, experience, or expertise that can improve the assessment and evaluation of the matter.

Perhaps the risk is so significant that even if the directors have confidence in management and its ability to handle the situation, they should be aware of the risk and formally approve related actions.

Or, perhaps by talking about a specific risk the board can gain insights into and confidence in management's ability to manage risk in general.

But, just because something is assessed as a "high risk" should not mean that the board needs to spend more time than delivers value talking about it.

****

In the same vein, when should the board discuss risk? Should there be a risk committee of the board?

The regulators seem to be clear on this: they like the idea of a committee that focuses on risk. They also like to see a formal focus (typically by the compensation committee of the board) on risks related to executive compensation (i.e., whether the compensation structure might induce executives to act in their own short-term interests at the expense of the company's longer term interests).

Of course, the regulators are thinking almost exclusively of risk that can have a negative effect on the organization. But, there is value in having one committee, either the risk or audit committee (or a joint audit and risk committee), that is charged with oversight of the risk management system.

Risk should be discussed at the same time as strategy[94], at the same time as potential acquisitions or major projects, as an integral part of the review of performance, and at the same time as operational and financial budgets, forecasts, and projections.

In other words, risk should be embedded into the fabric and the operations of the board and its committees.

Board Risk Competence

Should the board include individuals who might be called "risk management experts", in the same way as they should have one or more "financial experts" on the audit committee?

Just as I believe every manager should understand the management of risk and be considered a 'risk manager', so should every board member – at least in an ideal world.

Today, not every director has a sufficient understanding of risk and risk management. But these are smart people and I don't think it would be hard for them to develop a sufficient understanding (with the help of the CRO) to challenge management and gain comfort that the organization as a whole manages risk effectively. After all, while the board may be ultimately responsible for the management of risk, they should be able to delegate much of that to management – in the same way that they delegate to and rely on management for financial reporting and daily operations – with periodic reviews to confirm that is being done effectively.

---

[94] I heard a panel presentation where one of the panelists was a member of the board of the Hudson Bay Company (a Canadian company). He related how that company did not have separate strategy and risk meetings. Recognizing that they should be inextricably linked, the Hudson Bay discussed strategies and risks to their achievement at the same regular meetings of the board.

I like the expression, "noses in, fingers out". It is frequently used in discussions of the board's role as an oversight function ("noses in") that should not try to micromanage and run the business ("fingers out"). I think the expression goes further. The members of the board need to try to sense, through listening to and watching the executive management team, whether they are performing to their expectations. Sometimes, a world-class director will ask a question, not for the answer but to see how the executive responds. Does risk management smell good?

The board does not have the time, information, resources, or constant access to the organization to provide oversight of the risk-taking that is happening every day across the organization. It cannot supervise and monitor the quality of decisions. It has to rely on executive management, but test their comfort level in the organization's management of risk at every meeting (i.e., "trust and verify"). Some high level understanding of risk management is required for that, but what they need most is an understanding that the consideration of risk should be integrated into every one of their discussions, every proposal they approve.

Board Risk Information

One of the key points in the NACD report is that the board needs information if it is to provide effective risk oversight: "5. Work with management to understand and agree on the types (and format) of risk information the board requires".

Surveys have consistently found that many[95] directors are dissatisfied with the information they receive, not only with respect to risk but also about the organization's strategies!

One of the great aspects of the NACD guidance is that it starts with "Understand the company's key drivers of success". Unfortunately, surveys indicate that many directors do *not* have a sufficient understanding of the organization they serve and how it creates value for its stakeholders. Many don't understand the strategies that have been (supposedly) approved by the board.

---

[95] In their *2014 Annual Corporate Directors Survey*, PwC reported that "29% are either dissatisfied with or don't receive any information about competitor initiatives and strategy".

Without a solid understanding of the organization's ability to create and deliver value, and the strategies and objectives designed to do so, it is not possible to challenge management's representations of the more significant risks to the achievement of objectives. In fact, it is doubtful that a board that lacks this essential foundation will have the ability to assess whether management has effective processes for delivering performance and managing related risks.

The board needs to work with management to ensure it receives the periodic and continuing information required to:

- Understand how the organization creates value for its stakeholders and measures success

- Understand the organization's strategies and objectives and why they were chosen

- Understand how management monitors performance and risk on a continuing basis

- Obtain the assurance it needs that management's processes can be relied upon

- Be informed when risks to the achievement of organizational objectives are outside acceptable levels – especially when board action is required

The board should not wait for management to provide it with the information that the executives want the board to have.

The board should listen to recommendations about the information it will receive, but demand the information it needs when those recommendations are not acceptable.

Board Approval of Risk Levels

The regulators agree that the board should establish or approve the levels of risk they want management to take – referring to risk that may harm asset values, etc.

- ASX guidance: "It is the role of the board to set the risk appetite for the entity".

- The Singapore code: "[the Board] should determine the nature and extent of the significant risks which the Board is willing to take in achieving its strategic objectives", and "The Board should determine the company's levels of risk tolerance."

- The UK Corporate Governance Code issued in May 2010: "the Board is responsible for determining the nature and extent of the significant risks it is willing to take in achieving its strategic objectives".

While the regulators don't all use the same risk language, most prefer 'risk appetite', which is typically defined using the COSO ERM definition: "Risk appetite is the amount of risk, on a broad level, an organization is willing to accept in pursuit of stakeholder value."

I can understand that the board may want to influence what management will consider an acceptable level of risk. Where the risk relates to a financial position that is easy to quantify, establishing 'risk appetite' is also relatively easy. But, as I will discuss in the chapter on risk evaluation, establishing risk appetite for all potential effects of uncertainty is far less easy.

ISO 31000:2009 talks about risk criteria against which risks are evaluated to determine whether to accept or modify them. I prefer this term because of the way 'risk appetite' is too often considered a single number for all risks or a category of risk. In practice, decision-makers need guidance at their level that is meaningful to the decision they are making and the risk they will create or modify – more on this later.

I believe the board and management should agree which risks require board-level attention and, where it makes sense, agree on limits. That is very much an exercise that will be specific to the organization, its regulatory environment, its business sector, its risk capacity, and more. Jim DeLoach of Protiviti comments: "This is essentially the approach I take with risk appetite, using assertions that are relevant to the organization and its circumstances, resulting in strategic, operational and financial parameters within which the organization should operate."

So, I can accept (subject to the discussion in the risk evaluation chapter) that "the Board is responsible for determining the nature and extent of the significant risks it is willing to take in achieving its strategic objectives".

Chapter 10: Risk culture and framework

When regulators and others performed their post-mortems on the 'Great Recession' of 2008, in particular the failures of financial services companies, 'culture' was very often blamed. Risk culture has since been blamed for additional failures, including the "London Whale" (at JP Morgan Chase) and BP Deepwater Horizon disasters.

> Analysis of the impact of the financial crisis and the role of ERM by the US Risk and Insurance Management Society (RIMS) showed that risk culture issues were at the centre of the failure of major banks[96]" – Alex Hindson, CRO at Amlin AG and former President of the Institute of Risk Management

> The strategy set by the Board from the creation of the new Group sowed the seeds of its destruction. HBOS set a strategy for aggressive, asset-led growth across divisions over a sustained period. This involved accepting more risk across all divisions of the Group. Although many of the strengths of the two brands within HBOS largely persisted at branch level, the strategy created a new culture in the higher echelons of the bank. This culture was brash, underpinned by a belief that the growing market share was due to a special set of skills which HBOS possessed and which its competitors lacked."- Parliamentary Commission on Banking Standards, 2013)

> ...the leaders of industry must collectively procure a visible and substantive change in the culture of our institutions, so as fundamentally to convince the world once again that they are businesses which can be relied on." Marcus Agius, chairman of Barclays (FT.com, 2010)

> Absent major crises, and given the remarkable financial returns available from deepwater reserves, the business culture succumbed to a false sense of security. The Deepwater Horizon disaster exhibits the costs of a culture of complacency... There are recurring themes of missed warning signals, failure to share information, and a general lack of appreciation for the risks involved. In the view of the Commission, these findings highlight the importance of organizational culture and a consistent commitment to safety by industry, from the

---

[96] *Developing a risk culture*, Risk Management Professional, December 2010

highest management levels on down." (National Commission on the BP Deepwater Horizon Oil Spill and Offshore Drilling, 2011)

This is clearly an important topic. *Risk Culture in Financial Organisations*[97] and *Risk culture: Under the Microscope Guidance for Boards*[98]are useful references and several of the consulting firms (such as McKinsey, Deloitte, PwC, KPMG, and Protiviti[99]) and the risk management professional associations (such as RIMS, the risk management society) have studied and written about risk culture as well.

What exactly is Risk Culture?

This is how it is described in *Risk culture: Under the Microscope Guidance for Boards*:

Risk culture is a term describing the values, beliefs, knowledge and understanding about risk shared by a group of people with a common purpose, in particular the employees of an organisation or of teams or groups within an organisation. This applies whether the organisations are private companies, public bodies or not-for-profits and wherever they are in the world.

All organisations need to take risks to achieve their objectives. The prevailing risk culture within an organisation can make it significantly better or worse at managing these risks. Risk culture significantly affects the capability to take strategic risk decisions and deliver on performance promises.

Organisations with inappropriate risk cultures will inadvertently find themselves allowing activities that are totally at odds with stated policies and procedures or operating completely outside these policies.

An inappropriate risk culture means not only that certain individuals or teams will undertake these activities but that the rest of the organisation ignores, condones or does not see what is going on. At

---

[97] By Michael Power, Simon Ashby, and Tommaso Palermo, published by (among others) the London School of Economics in 2012
[98] Published by the Institute of Risk Management in 2012. I was a minor contributor.
[99] *Establishing and Nurturing an Effective Risk Culture*, 2014

best this will hamper the achievement of strategic, tactical and operational goals. At worst it will lead to serious reputational and financial damage."

That first sentence starts to help me understand what risk culture is. But I need more to see beyond the words to a meaning that has relevance in an organization.

An article by John Michael Farrell and Angela Hoon, *What's Your Company's Risk Culture*, published in Directorship on May 12, 2009 is very helpful. Here are some excerpts:

Part of the challenge in addressing the issue is obtaining a clear understanding of what is meant by 'risk culture'. It can be defined as the system of values and behaviors present throughout an organization that shape risk decisions. Risk culture influences the decisions of management and employees, even if they are not consciously weighing risks and benefits.

One element of risk culture is the degree to which individuals understand that risk and compliance rules apply to everyone as they pursue their business goals. To start, that requires a common understanding of the organization and its business purpose (i.e., their raison d'être). Today, some seem to have lost sight of those business goals, forgetting that they serve the company and shareholders, and not the other way around.

A company's risk culture is a critical element that can ensure that "doing the right thing" wins over "doing whatever it takes." In fact, in a recent KPMG International survey of almost 500 bank executives, almost half (48 percent) of respondents cited risk culture as a leading contributor to the credit crisis. Clearly, those financial institutions that have a history of strong risk culture have weathered the storm best.

Although risk culture has become a fundamental building block of good ERM practices, many companies show evidence of deficiencies in this area. For instance, more than half (58 percent) of corporate Board members and internal auditors surveyed by KPMG said that their company's employees had little or no understanding of how risk exposures should be assessed for likelihood and impact. One-third of those same respondents also said that key leaders in their organization had no formal risk management training or guidance, with only 16 percent receiving at least annual training.

What this is telling me is that a strong risk culture is all about managers and decision-makers (a) knowing what is expected of them when it comes to risk management, and (b) behaving the "right" way (taking the desired level of the right risks).

The article continues:

Having a strong risk culture means that employees know what the company stands for, the boundaries within which they can operate, and that they can discuss and debate openly which risks should be taken in order to achieve the company's long-term strategic goals.

A strong risk culture can be built over time, but it also has to be inspired. Management's actions as well as consistent, ongoing communication around ethics and risk management become the first steps to instilling such a culture because it will demonstrate that inappropriate behavior will not be tolerated. Board members can help instill such a culture by asking the right questions and providing an outside perspective on what is/is not working. Once leadership starts on the right path—and stays on it—the organization will slowly but surely follow.

Risk culture: Under the Microscope Guidance for Boards agrees:

An effective risk culture is one that enables and rewards individuals and groups for taking the right risks in an informed manner.

A successful risk culture would include:

1. A distinct and consistent tone from the top from the board and senior management in respect of risk taking and avoidance (and also consideration of tone at all levels)

2. A commitment to ethical principles, reflected in a concern with the ethical profile of individuals and the application of ethics and the consideration of wider stakeholder positions in decision making

3. A common acceptance through the organisation of the importance of continuous management of risk, including clear accountability for and ownership of specific risks and risk areas

4. Transparent and timely risk information flowing up and down the organisation with bad news rapidly communicated without fear of blame

5. Encouragement of risk event reporting and whistle blowing, actively seeking to learn from mistakes and near misses

6. No process or activity too large or too complex or too obscure for the risks to be readily understood

7. Appropriate risk taking behaviours rewarded and encouraged and inappropriate behaviours challenged and sanctioned

8. Risk management skills and knowledge valued, encouraged and developed, with a properly resourced risk management function and widespread membership of and support for professional bodies. Professional qualifications supported as well as technical training

9. Sufficient diversity of perspectives, values and beliefs to ensure that the status quo is consistently and rigorously challenged

10. Alignment of culture management with employee engagement and people strategy to ensure that people are supportive socially but also strongly focused on the task in hand.

In April 2014, the Financial Stability Board (FSB) published *Guidance on Supervisory Interaction with Financial Institutions on Risk Culture: A Framework for Assessing Risk Culture*. I believe it is an excellent source for those seeking to understand this phenomenon called risk culture. It says:

Weaknesses in risk culture are often considered a root cause of the global financial crisis, headline risk and compliance events. A financial institution's risk culture plays an important role in influencing the actions and decisions taken by individuals within the institution and in shaping the institution's attitude toward its stakeholders, including its supervisors.

A sound risk culture consistently supports appropriate risk awareness, behaviours and judgements about risk-taking within a strong risk governance framework. A sound risk culture bolsters effective risk management, promotes sound risk-taking, and ensures that emerging risks or risk-taking activities beyond the institution's risk appetite are recognised, assessed, escalated and addressed in a timely manner.

A sound risk culture should emphasise throughout the institution the importance of ensuring that: (i) an appropriate risk-reward balance consistent with the institution's risk appetite is achieved when taking on risks; (ii) an effective system of controls commensurate with the scale and complexity of the financial institution is properly put in place; (iii) the quality of risk models, data accuracy, capability of available tools to accurately measure risks, and justifications for risk taking can be challenged, and (iv) all limit breaches, deviations from established policies, and operational incidents are thoroughly followed up with proportionate disciplinary actions when necessary.

Risk culture, as well as corporate culture, evolves over time in relation to the events that affect the institution's history (such as mergers and acquisitions) and to the external context within which the institution operates. Sub-cultures within institutions may exist depending on the different contexts within which parts of the institution operate. However sub-cultures should adhere to the high-level values and elements that support the institution's overall risk culture.

First and foremost, it should be expected that employees in all parts of the institution conduct business in a legal and ethical manner. An environment that promotes integrity should be created across the institution as a whole, including focusing on fair outcomes for customers.

The FSB paper outlines a number of features of a strong risk culture that are similar to those identified by *Under the Microscope Guidance for Boards*. However, I find these symptoms of a poorly functioning risk culture more revealing (from *Developing a risk culture* by Alex Hindson, published in Risk Management Professional, December 2010).

- Leadership sends inconsistent or unclear messages on acceptable levels of risk

- Risk is perceived to be managed intuitively and not discussed in making decisions

- Provided business results are delivered, few questions get asked regarding what might go wrong

- There is little or no sanction for those taking inappropriate levels of risk

In other words, people either don't know what the rules of the risk game are or don't believe that they really mean what they say: those who ignore or violate the rewards go unpunished, perhaps even rewarded for "thinking out of the box," having an "entrepreneurial spirit", or "doing what it takes".

How is this different from what I said in earlier chapters about the board, the CEO, and the rest of the executive team not only embracing but embodying risk management?

If leadership truly believes in the value of risk management as an integral part of how you set strategy and objectives, make decisions, and run the organization, you will have an effective risk culture. It helps to have this enshrined in corporate policies and standards, but policies and standards influence behavior far less than people would like to think. My view: policies and standards help you fire somebody who violates them, but they rarely change human behavior.

The responsibilities of the board in providing oversight of risk management (in fact, oversight of management in general) should include:

- Making it clear that mature risk management is essential to the effective management of the organization. Requiring that executive management move the management of risk up the maturity curve to the level appropriate for the organization, including challenging management if they have anything less than the highest level; asking that the CEO provide a formal report at least annually with his assessment of the quality of the risk management system; ensuring that the CRO has the necessary capabilities and resources to be effective; and, obtaining assurance from the CRO (or CEO if there is no CRO) that risk management is embraced and embodied by management across the organization.

- Setting the tone, the expectations for behavior, including not only complying with an ethical code of conduct but putting the interests of the organization as a whole ahead of those of the individual manager, team, or business unit.

- Walking the talk, not only in their own behavior but in their challenging of management to do the same. Holding management accountable, with consequences, when they fail to demonstrate appropriate behaviors or condone inappropriate behavior by their subordinates.

- Requiring that internal audit provide a formal assessment of not only internal control but risk management on at least an annual basis

As noted above, executives, managers, and decision-makers do not consistently demonstrate desired behaviors. They don't always make risk decisions that are in the best interests of the organization – and often that is not due to an ethical failure as much as it is due to ignorance.

It is not sufficient to pay occasional attention to this issue. Turnover among executives, managers, and decision-makers is constant. Business conditions and personal situations also change constantly, putting opportunity in front of those who might be might be tempted to bypass what they rationalize as bureaucratic red-tape and take a level or type of risk that is unacceptable to leadership.

It is easy to make the mistake of thinking that an organization has a single risk culture. In fact, different groups and locations within an organization can vary substantially. That is especially true for global organizations, where local values and ways of doing business can lead to significant differences in attitudes towards decision-making and risk-taking.

Management, with leadership from the CRO, should have controls in place that:

- Provide guidance to decision-makers that informs them of desired behavior, including the consideration of risk as they make decisions and run the business

- Ensure that decision-makers are familiar with and understand the guidance

- Provide decision-makers with the tools and advice they need for decision-making

- Ensure appropriate review of risk decisions by senior management and, as necessary, the board

- Reward appropriate behavior and ensure that those who behave poorly are disciplined

- Detect inappropriate behavior

- Ensure action is taken when a more pervasive situation is detected, as this may indicate a failure of leadership, communication, and/or controls

Risk Management Framework

Risk culture is part of the *risk management framework*, as described by ISO 31000:2009. ISO defines the framework as the "set of components that provide the foundations and organizational arrangements for designing, implementing, monitoring, reviewing and continually improving risk management throughout the organization."

Unfortunately, the ISO standard is not very effective in describing what those components are[100]. So, I will put that aside and share my list of what the framework includes:

1. A mandate from the board and executive management; the embracing and embodying of risk management by the board and executive team from the CEO on down

2. A risk management policy designed to inform the organization of expectations in the management of risk, including the consideration of risk in strategy-setting, performance management and monitoring, decision-making, forecasting, project management, and so on. The policy should make it clear that every manager and decision-maker is responsible for the management of risk, not only to their own and team objectives but to the objectives of others and of the organization as a whole. The policy should also explain that individuals who make decisions and cause risk to be outside acceptable levels will be disciplined; it may mandate that certain risk-related situations be reported to senior management, the CRO, and the board as appropriate. The policy may include a section on the role of the CRO

---

[100] In my opinion, the text is more applicable to the initial implementation of risk management than describing what effective risk management looks like.

3. As mentioned above, there should be controls to ensure everybody understands these expectations

4. The "how" of risk management: the processes, systems, responsibilities, and reporting

5. The periodic review, assessment, and improvement of the risk management system

Does every organization need a risk management policy? I believe that will depend on the organization's culture (for example, is everything dictated by formal policies, such as in a bank) and what they need to be effective. As I said before, policies rarely change behavior. But they do establish expectations and when management reinforces those expectations through their daily behavior, when they reward desired behavior and discipline inappropriate behavior, employees are more likely to follow them.

I like the BHP Billiton and CQUniversity policies included in Appendices A and B. They are fairly high level; they set expectations in general but don't describe responsibilities, processes, or systems in detail. The risk management policy at SAP goes further; it "governs how we handle risk in line with the Company's risk appetite and defines a methodology that is applied uniformly across all parts of the Group. The policy stipulates who is responsible for conducting risk management activities and defines reporting and monitoring structures".

When I ran risk management at Business Objects, we didn't have a risk management policy! This was an entrepreneurial company that relied on its management team to follow the lead of the CEO and embrace and embody the management of risk. Our CEO, John Schwarz, made it clear that he looked to his management team to manage risk to the achievement of their and the organization's objectives, and I was able to form a management risk council with the active participation of several of his direct reports.

While there was no formal risk management system per se before I took on a leadership role, the company had a legacy of effective risk management to build on. Our process for developing new products was disciplined and gave serious consideration to the identification and management of risk to the successful development, launch, and acceptance of our products by the market[101].

I believe an organization with world-class risk management will not only have a framework that is tailored for its specific needs (recognizing that may change over time) but a culture consistent with that framework. In other words, the members of the organization will believe in the integration of risk into how they manage the business and do so in accordance with the expectations of leadership.

Management and the board will not rely entirely on their trust in employees, but will have the control structure that not only provides reasonable assurance that employees will behave appropriately but detect and report any instances when they fail to do so.

---

[101] The Project Management Institute certification (Project Management Professional) requires risk management skills – project risk management is one of its ten "knowledge areas". PMI defines risk as ""an uncertain event or condition that, if it occurs, has a positive or negative effect on one or more project objectives such as scope, schedule, cost, or quality."

Chapter 11: Risk identification and monitoring

"There are none so blind as those that will not see[102]".

You will not be able to identify risks if you are not looking for them. Since risks change constantly, you need to be looking constantly.

Risk identification is both a periodic exercise and a continuous activity. At regular intervals, management should assess the situation and identify the risks between where it is and where it wants to be. In ISO, this is the "risk identification" step in the risk management process. In COSO, it is the "event identification" component.

> ISO: The organization should identify sources of risk, areas of impacts, events (including changes in circumstances) and their causes and their potential consequences. The aim of this step is to generate a comprehensive list of risks based on those events that might create, enhance, prevent, degrade, accelerate or delay the achievement of objectives. It is important to identify the risks associated with not pursuing an opportunity. Comprehensive identification is critical, because a risk that is not identified at this stage will not be included in further analysis.

> COSO: Management identifies potential events that, if they occur, will affect the entity, and determines whether they represent opportunities or whether they might adversely affect the entity's ability to implement strategy and achieve objectives. Events with negative impact represent risks, which require management's assessment and response. Events with positive impact represent opportunities, which management channels back into the strategy and objective-setting processes. When identifying events, management considers a variety of internal and external factors that may give rise to risks and opportunities, in the context of the full scope of the organization.

Both ISO and COSO seem to see this as something that is done at a regular interval, say monthly or quarterly. But in fact, it should be done every time a decision is being considered (as discussed earlier). Before an

---

[102] A proverb that has been attributed to John Heywood in 1546 and is similar to Jeremiah 5:21: "Hear now this, O foolish people, and without understanding; which have eyes, and see not; which have ears, and hear not"

intelligent decision can be made, it is necessary to identify, analyze, and evaluate the risks (both positive and negative) that can happen for each option.

Top-Down or Bottom-Up

When you consider the objectives and identify risks to their achievement, you are following a top-down approach. This is my preference, but there is also a need for a bottoms-up approach.

New risks may be identified at any moment due to the changing nature of the business environment, especially related to the organization's use and dependency on technology. In recent years, we have seen the emergence of concerns over social media, BYOD (bring your own device), cyber warfare units of criminal syndicates and foreign nations (not only attacking military and political targets, but also successfully hacking banks and other corporation's systems to steal information for economic or other advantage)[103], and more.

Each of these new sources of risk needs to be assessed. If we look at the first part of the COSO and ISO language above, they qualify:

- "Management identifies potential events that, if they occur, will affect the entity" (COSO)

- "The organization should identify sources of risk, areas of impacts, events (including changes in circumstances) and their causes and their potential consequences" (ISO)

Unfortunately, many stop there. They identify these as risks to the organization without asking whether they are critical to the achievement of the objectives of the organization. Both the COSO and ISO discussions accurately express this need:

---

[103] In fact, nobody's systems should be considered safe if they are connected directly or indirectly to the Internet. Almost every nation now has an organized cyberwarfare unit; the ability to defend new attacks lags the ability to launch them; and, intrusions are often not detected for months (the J.P. Morgan Chase 2014 intrusion being a prime example).

- "...and determines whether they represent opportunities or whether they might adversely affect the entity's ability to implement strategy and achieve objectives." (COSO)

- "The aim of this step is to generate a comprehensive list of risks based on those events that might create, enhance, prevent, degrade, accelerate or delay the achievement of objectives." (ISO)

New risks may seem very important at first blush but, on further examination, are assessed as less than critical to the stated (and implied[104]) objectives of the organization.

IT Risk

I have worked with a great many IT executives and IT auditors over the years. Several are excellent in understanding risk, but too many focus on so-called "IT risk". I often quote a good friend, Jay Taylor[105], who said "there is no such thing as IT risk – only business risk".

Many "IT risk assessments" look at risk to such concerns as systems availability, data protection, and so on. But these are the IT organization's objectives and not the organization's objectives. What is necessary is to upgrade the risk assessment to considering how, for example, a failure to maintain systems availability would affect business operations and, then, whether any critical organizational objectives may be 'at risk'. For example, a failure to maintain acceptable levels of systems availability might affect the organization's ability to process sales orders, fulfil those orders, and bill customers. In turn, this could impact organizational objectives around revenue and earnings, customer satisfaction, cash flow, and reputation. The effect on each of these business objectives should be evaluated to determine whether the IT risk is acceptable when viewed through the lens of the affected business objectives. Management should also assess whether the aggregated effect on multiple objectives is

---

[104] Many objectives, such as employee safety and compliance, are not formally stated. However, they may be considered as implied objectives, necessary for the continued health of the organization. In fact, they may actually be necessary to achieve the stated objectives of the organization as a failure to achieve these unstated objectives may disrupt operations, tie up capital and management attention, and otherwise impede performance.

[105] At that time, Jay was responsible for IT auditing at General Motors.

sufficient to warrant mitigation, even if none of those business risks individually exceed acceptable criteria. (Business judgment and common sense may indicate that the cost of mitigation is low relative to the aggregated business, considering all business objectives.)

In 2009, ISACA published *The RiskIT Framework*[106]. It says:

> IT risk is business risk—specifically, the business risk associated with the use, ownership, operation, involvement, influence and adoption of IT within an enterprise. It consists of IT-related events that could potentially impact the business. It can occur with both uncertain frequency and magnitude, and it creates challenges in meeting strategic goals and objectives.

Unfortunately, those who stop at "IT risk" without making the upgrade to business risk often focus on issues that are marginally important (if at all) to the success of the organization as a whole, and don't commit the resources to areas where they are critical to organizational strategies. (This often reflects an inability to flow corporate objectives down to IT.)

In my first year as vice president of internal audit at a technology company[107], the head of security[108] and the IT executive responsible for information security asked for a meeting. They said that they needed my support to persuade the senior executives that they needed to encrypt the hard drives on their laptops. They explained the obvious: the senior executives' laptops held critical customer, financial, and operating information including the company's strategies and plans, as well as financial forecasts, product cost information, and more. At that time, the technology to encrypt hard drives was not inexpensive and it would make the executives' use of the applications on those devices more difficult. I could see why the management team was balking at the idea, both from a cost and an ease-of-use perspective, when the benefit was only to limit the potential damage should their device be lost or stolen – even though that happened with disturbing regularity!

I asked the two managers if they had done a risk assessment. They said they had. I was more than a little doubtful and asked whether they had

---

[106] *ITRisk* is now incorporated into COBIT 5.
[107] This was in the early years of this century.
[108] This included physical security and executive protection.

assessed all the risks relating to technology within the business. They said that not only had they completed a full IT risk assessment, but that the potential for somebody with technical acumen to obtain a lost or stolen laptop, and use the confidential information it retained, was the top risk.

When they said this, I asked if their risk assessment had considered the fact that the organization's diverse global operations used multiple financial systems (they had everything ever invented), which were cobbled together with Excel spreadsheets for financial reporting and to consolidate operating information. Didn't they think that was a significant business risk? I also asked whether they believed the company's network was secure, given that they had yet to implement any intrusion detection or prevention systems.

In short, they had not stepped back and thought about whether the risk they had identified was significant to the business as a whole and its overall objectives. It looked important, sounded important, but was only a minor issue[109].

A world-class organization reads, listens, and otherwise identifies new risks using a bottoms-up approach in addition to a top-down process. For example, it might receive a communication from an employee warning that persistent product safety issues are being ignored by management. It then asks which business objectives (stated or otherwise) might be affected and then follows the appropriate risk management process with leadership from risk owners[110].

Facilitated Workshops

One of the best ways to identify risks is through a workshop. This is a technique that is well-researched and highly-effective, not only in identifying but assessing risks.

My first experience with a risk workshop was before anybody referred to them as risk workshops[111]. In about 1983, I was a vice president in the

---

[109] This experience triggered an audit of overall information security risk assessment, structure, organization, and planning. The assessment drove significant change.

[110] As defined in ISO 31000, a risk owner is the "person or entity with the accountability and authority to manage a risk".

internal audit department at Home Savings of America. One of my responsibilities was leading the IT audit team and I was concerned about the access that application developers had to the production system. Senior IT management didn't believe it was a significant source of risk, so with their permission I convened a workshop that included several business and IT managers. I modeled the workshop on what I had read about Joint Application Design (JAD), which had become popular over the prior decade[112]. We had a lively and productive discussion that identified a number of risks to the business, each of which we assessed as a group. The facilitated risk workshop is now the mainstay of many risk functions.

What Needs to Go Right?

Somebody[113] once suggested that while risk practitioners are often asked "what could go wrong", a better question is usually "what needs to go right".

I really like this question.

It's especially useful in turning assumptions into a list of risks and related actions.

Managers at every level make assumptions when they put plans together. Unfortunately, even if they deem them solid and reasonable, they don't take every action appropriate to ensuring that reality matches their hopes – and assumptions are only hopes if actions are not taken to realize them. If, instead, they look at each of their assumptions, assess them (in terms of their likelihood of happening as they desire), determine whether the likelihood of their assumptions not coming to pass is acceptable or not, take action to mitigate the risk of their not occurring – and then continue

---

[111] The terms "risk assessment workshop" and "risk identification workshop" are also used.
[112] *JAD Guidelines*, from Knowledge Structures, Inc.: "Joint Application Development (JAD) sessions are highly structured, facilitated workshops that bring together customer decision makers and IS staff to produce high-quality deliverables in a short time period. The original term "Joint Application Design" has evolved to "Joint Application Development" because these sessions are now used effectively throughout the software development cycle."
[113] Probably Grant Purdy

to monitor the risk – there is a far greater likelihood that their plans will be successful.

A world-class organization sets its strategies and objectives and asks "what needs to go right". Then and only then can it successfully cascade objectives down and across the organization. This is the only way to ensure everybody whose actions are necessary to achieve objectives knows they own those tasks and will be held responsible and accountable for them.

The ISO 31000:2009 global risk management standard explains that the risk management process it describes can be applied to the achievement of objectives at any level of the organization. This is useful when the achievement of organizational objectives is cascaded down to objectives at executive, business unit, location, team, and individual levels. At each level, the owner of the objective can and should ask "what needs to go right" and "what could go wrong". He identifies and manages the risks to his objectives, which are also risks to the achievement of the organization's objectives.

Continuous Risk Identification

Neither COSO nor ISO pay sufficient attention[114], in my opinion, to the need for *continuous* risk identification. By the way, I am not talking about continuous risk *assessment* – I will cover that in the next chapter. I am talking about identifying risks that had not previously been identified.

In a famous 2002 U.S. Defense Department new briefing, then Secretary of Defense Donald Rumsfeld said "Reports that say that something hasn't happened are always interesting to me, because as we know, there are known knowns; there are things we know we know. We also know there are known unknowns; that is to say we know there are some things we do not know. But there are also unknown unknowns -- the ones we don't know we don't know. And if one looks throughout the history of our country and other free countries, it is the latter category that tend to be the difficult ones."

---

[114] An argument may be made that COSO includes continuous risk identification when it talks about key risk indicators, and that ISO covers it under the monitoring step in the risk management process.

Rumsfeld got what he deserved for this erudite but impenetrable comment: laughter and scorn. While there are some scientists who talk this way, common people – the people he was talking to – don't. (This reminds me of risk managers who talk about "stochastic modeling" or, as I found in an article on flood risk, "continuous probability density". Common people, whether on the street or in the boardroom, don't talk this way.)

Since then, risk practitioners and commentators have started to use the Rumsfeld quote to make a point. I guess I am one of the latest.

Uncertainty and its effect, risk, are clearly *unknown*. Sometimes, we know what might happen but cannot be certain whether it will happen and what its effect might be. These are *"known* unknowns'. We can make an intelligent assessment of their impact and likelihood.

But there are some uncertainties between where we are and where we want to be that we have not yet seen. They may be out of view, or we may be looking in the wrong direction.

For example, when I was at Business Objects our primary competitors were Cognos and Hyperion. We were a clear number one in the business analytics market, far ahead of either of our rivals. However, we knew very well that we were all minnows compared to the great software sharks: IBM, Microsoft, Oracle, and SAP. We knew that at some point, one or more of these predators might want to fish in our waters. We didn't know that they would, and we hoped that we had many years before they did. We treasured our independence.

The risk that a shark would enter our waters and put their massive weight (i.e., dollars) behind one of our competitors was known. It was a known unknown. If they did jump in our small pool, the consequences could be severe. We identified this as a risk in our risk management process and the decision was to watch carefully so we could respond should the event seem likely to occur.

In February 2007, Oracle announced that it was acquiring Hyperion. The first shark had struck! Now we had to decide how to respond. One option was to carry on as normal. But then the other sharks came a-calling. The board and management weighed the options of staying independent or agreeing to be acquired by one of the giants. After negotiations with several suitors, the company decided to sell itself to SAP. In October 2007,

IBM announced that it would acquire Cognos and SAP announced that it was acquiring Business Objects.

Although we had very little insight in 2006 whether any of the sharks would come after us, this was a known unknown – a risk we identified and discussed at management and board level.

Since then, the analytics market has changed. New companies have sprung up and offer different forms of analytics, such as semantic analysis. In addition, artificial intelligence (sometimes referred to as machine learning and led by IBM's Watson) is starting to gain ground as an analytics technology. All of these are threats to SAP BusinessObjects'[115] dominance.

In 2006, and even in 2009 when I left risk management at Business Objects/SAP, none of these was on our radar. I would consider these unknown unknowns.

So, how do you design your risk management system to identify what is unseen and unknown?

My approach at Business Objects was to make sure we had people looking in the most likely directions where a risk could surface. The CEO assigned executives the responsibility for keeping their eyes and ears open in specific areas and letting us all know when the initial signs started to appear.

I don't know that there is much more that you can do. Some believe that monitoring software can help, but that will only identify what you tell it to look for – by definition, known unknowns.

The key is to know that these risks are real, even if you can't see them. So we need to keep our eyes peeled and our ears to the ground so that we can identify them as quickly as possible. Then they can be analyzed.

---

[115] Business Objects was renamed SAP BusinessObjects when the acquisition was completed.

Chapter 12: Risk analysis

I'm not a fan of either COSO or ISO when it comes to this stage in the risk management process. The ISO 31000:2009 global management standard includes risk identification, risk analysis, and risk evaluation in "risk assessment". But, there is neither explanation nor reason I can see for combining the three. The COSO *Enterprise Risk Management – Integrated Framework* has event identification (instead of risk identification – as discussed previously) and combines risk analysis and evaluation into risk assessment. Personally, I find that more interesting but will deal with each separately.

The risk analysis step is where the level of risk[116] is determined. The risk evaluation step is where the risk is compared to risk criteria and a decision made whether to accept the risk or act to mitigate it.

The ISO description of risk analysis makes it seem much simpler than it really is.

> Risk analysis involves consideration of the causes and sources of risk, their positive and negative consequences, and the likelihood that those consequences can occur. Factors that affect consequences and likelihood should be identified. Risk is analyzed by determining consequences and their likelihood, and other attributes of the risk. An event can have multiple consequences and can affect multiple objectives. Existing controls and their effectiveness and efficiency should also be taken into account.

There are a few significant differences between the COSO description of risk assessment and the ISO description, above. This is how COSO describes the risk assessment component.

> Risk assessment allows an entity to consider the extent to which potential events[117] have an impact on achievement of objectives.

---

[116] ISO 31000:2009 defines level of risk as "magnitude of a risk or combination of risks, expressed in terms of the combination of consequences and their likelihood".

[117] A strong argument can be made that "events" are not the only source of risk. I think that talking about events is fine as long as there is an understanding that risk is also created or modified by decisions. It is also a fact of life that sometimes the situation has changed (and the risk level has changed) without any apparent

Management assesses events from two perspectives – likelihood and impact – and normally uses a combination of qualitative and quantitative methods. The positive and negative impact of potential events should be examined, individually or by category, across the entity. Risks are assessed on both an inherent and a residual basis.

The differences are very important indeed:

- ISO points out that there is more to analyze than likelihood and impact, which I will discuss in the next chapter, on risk evaluation.

- ISO also vitally says that a single event can have multiple consequences (which I am unable to find in the COSO Framework).

- COSO talks explicitly about inherent and residual risk, while ISO only implies that when it talks about considering existing controls.

A single event can and frequently does have multiple consequences, affecting multiple objectives. Those consequences can be a mixture of positive and negative (in terms of their effect on objectives). I cannot explain why COSO does not reference or, apparently, consider this. Frankly, I don't think ISO does enough to cover this either – there is little in the way of explanation or guidance.

In its risk assessment discussion, COSO (mis)uses the example of an earthquake in California from the perspective of an organization operating there. While COSO implies that a single number can be used to assess the level of risk following an earthquake, that view is misguided. A single earthquake can have the following consequences:

> ***Key point***: A single event can and frequently does have multiple consequences, affecting multiple objectives. Those consequences can be a mixture of positive and negative (in terms of their effect on objectives).

- Loss of life and injuries to company personnel

- Power outages that cause company operations to stop

- Fires that force employees to evacuate

event.

- Damage to equipment, inventory, and other assets
- Damage to the company's building
- Loss of the company network
- Loss of stored information
- An inability to perform accounting and operating functions on the company's systems
- A loss of communications with employees, customers, vendors, and so on
- Traffic disruption that prevents employees reaching the company's facilities
- Damage to hospitals and other necessary services
- Damage to the company's supply chain (unable to receive materials or ship product)
- Loss of customers
- Reputation damage
- An opportunity to provide services to those affected by the earthquake
- An opportunity to sell products to a competitor's customers when that competitor is affected by the disaster
- An opportunity to raise prices because demand outstrips supply
- An opportunity to acquire a business affected by the earthquake
- ...and more

Some key points:

1. An earthquake can have any or all of these consequences or more.

2. Each of these consequences can occur with varying levels of severity, duration, and so on. For example, the power outage could be limited to a few minutes or extend to days or weeks.

3. Each of these consequences, and each of the levels of severity for each consequence, has a different likelihood!

4. Some of the consequences are opportunities!

Let's examine this a little further, still using the earthquake example.

I live in the San Francisco Bay area, one that is famously prone to earthquakes. If we look at the possibility of an earthquake in the region, according to a 2007 forecast[118], there is a 63% probability of an earthquake of magnitude 6.7[119] or greater over the next 30 years. But there are many earthquake faults, the most likely of which at 31% to be the source of the earthquake is the Hayward-Rodgers Creek fault. That fault line is on the *east* side of the Bay and is quite a distance from the epicenter of the 1989 Loma Prieta Earthquake, which was near Santa Cruz and on the San Andreas fault line, *west* of the Bay.

So while there is a high chance of a severe earthquake in the next 30 years, we can't predict beyond a 31% level of confidence on which fault line it will happen – and we cannot predict where on the fault line it will happen.

The 63% forecast of a magnitude 6.7 or greater quake was over 30 years. When we are analyzing a risk, we need a much shorter time horizon. Unfortunately, the scientists have not yet been able to make short-term predictions, so our ability to estimate likelihood is going to be pretty much a guess.

But it's not a guess whether Northern California will have an earthquake of any magnitude. By 7:30am on December 17, 2014, there had already been 12 earthquakes that morning (the largest of which was 2.9); 81 in

---

[118] By the *2007 Working Group on California Earthquake Probabilities*

[119] On the Richter scale, this is rated as a "strong" earthquake. Average earthquake effects are described by the U.S. Geographical Survey as "Damage to a moderate number of well-built structures in populated areas. Earthquake-resistant structures survive with slight to moderate damage. Poorly designed structures receive moderate to severe damage. Felt in wider areas; up to hundreds of miles/kilometers from the epicenter. Strong to violent shaking in epicentral area. Death toll ranges from none to 25,000." The Northridge earthquake in 1994, which damaged homes, brought down bridges, and flattened apartments in my former neighborhood, was magnitude 6.7.

the previous 7 days; 397 in the past month; and 4,706 in the last year. So, it's 100% certain that my area will have an earthquake in the next year.

We did have earthquakes of some magnitude in 2014. There was a 6.8 with its epicenter near Eureka, California (less than 500 miles north of my home), and a 6.0 earthquake near Napa, California (less than 100 miles away). The Napa earthquake was felt in my neighborhood, but there was no damage here – only in the Napa-Sonoma area.

What does this mean?

- There is a slim chance of a severe earthquake in the next year that would affect my neighborhood in a significant way.

- It is almost 100% certain that there will be at least one slight earthquake in the next year, but it will not affect me beyond knowing that it happened (and maybe a short moment of "what's happening? It's an earthquake. Oh, it's over. We're OK.")

- There are possibilities of earthquakes of magnitudes between slight and severe, but there is no way we can predict when they will happen, how significant each will be, where their epicenters will be located, whether they will affect us, and to what extent they will affect us.

In other words, while we know we have 'earthquake risk', we cannot do more than estimate the likelihood of one that will have an effect on our operations.

If I were to analyze earthquake risk for my personal operations, I would ignore the hundreds of tiny earthquakes that I usually don't even feel and instead only assess the possibility of those that will have limited, moderate, or severe effects.

The *limited effect* earthquakes would be those with a magnitude of 4.0-5.9, described by the U.S. Geographical Survey as Light (4.0-4.9) or Moderate (5.0-5.9). While these would shake my work environment, damage to the structure would be slight to none. I would consider them because objects could fall off walls or shelves and injure people, cause water or sewer pipes and equipment to fail, and possibly lead to power disruption for a day or two.

In the last 20 years there have been about 45 light earthquakes in the San Francisco Bay area and 7 that were moderate; that's an average of more than 2 per year. Fortunately, there was no effect on me or my work environment, because I have measures in place to secure water pipes and equipment, and have only light items on the wall or shelves that are unlikely to injure anybody should they fall. There were no power outages in my area.

Taking into account, as suggested by ISO, the "existing controls and their effectiveness and efficiency", I consider this level of risk not only acceptable but also too slight to worry about. I would focus instead on larger earthquakes.

The *moderate effect* earthquakes I would define as those with a magnitude of 6.0-6.9, or Strong on the U.S. Geographical Survey scale. In the last 20 years, there have been 6 of these in the Bay area; none were close enough to my home to cause damage. However, there is a possibility that one might be close enough to affect us. The effect could be small to significant. My old home suffered a cracked chimney and an outside wall fell down in the 6.7 Northridge earthquake, when the epicenter was about ten miles away, while neighbors in adjacent street had so much damage their homes were torn down.

Even with a moderate earthquake, there is a range of potential effects. It is not practical to assess them all, so I will use my judgment and narrow it down to risks valued at $50,000, $100,000, and over $100,000. I have California earthquake insurance with a deductible of $103,000 so I will only consider the likelihood of earthquakes with effects of $50,000 or $100,000[120]. (Yes, there is a tiny chance of personal injury, but I am willing to accept that as a cost of living in this beautiful area of the world.)

Given my experience over the last 20 years in the Bay area and 10 years before that in Southern California, I am going to asess the likelihood of a $50,000 impact in the next year is 10% and the likelihood of a $100,000 impact is 2%.

---

[120] Using the COSO terms of inherent and residual risk, if my home is destroyed the inherent risk would be in excess of $1 million, but the residual risk is limited to the deductible on the insurance policy plus the disruption of my personal and professional life.

There have been 2 *severe* earthquakes over 6.9 in the last 20 years in the Bay area. One was in Eureka in 2004 and measured 7.2. The other was in Twentynine Palms, measured 7.0, and was nearly 500 miles away. I don't remember feeling either of them. However, severe earthquakes are definitely possible.

I am going to use my judgment and select an effect of $250,000 (the $103,000 insurance deductible plus my estimate of the cost of the disruption to my personal and professional life). I am assessing the likelihood of that effect at 1%.

To complete the picture, I have to consider the possibility of an earthquake that is so close and so severe that I or my wife are killed or disabled. I put that possibility at less than 1% (and hope it is zero).

So, with respect to 'earthquake risk', I have identified four: a 10% likelihood of a $50,000 impact; a 2% likelihood of $100,000 impact; a 1% likelihood of a $250,000 impact, and, a less than 1% likelihood of my or my wife's death or disability.

A similar exercise could be performed for other risk sources, such as currency risk.

If an English organization holds $500,000 (in U.S currency) in a bank account, the value of that account will vary as the dollar to pound currency exchange rate changes. The range within which the rate may vary, within a specified period of time, is huge. It may move in a very significantly positive way or a significantly negative way, and it may stay the same. On July 3, 2014, the pound was worth $1.715 (the high for the year); on December 17, 2014 it was worth $1.558. Over those 5½ months, it dropped about 10% in value. But, the pound started 2014 at $1.627, so over the first 6 months it rose about 5%

In addition, the bank account balance may vary over time between, say, $300,000 and $700,000. The effect of a change in the exchange rate will vary depending on how much U.S. currency is held.

How do you decide which impact(s) to consider? How should the level of risk be calculated?

Before leaving this section, there is another important issue to consider. With some risks, there is the potential for multiple events to have a cumulative effect. For example, a severe earthquake (such as in Nepal in

2015) may be followed by several aftershocks. Even though these are usually less significant in terms of their Richter scale rating, they strike an area that is already damaged. The consequences of the second wave of earthquakes can be far more than indicated by their Richter level. Similarly, when there is heavy rain that leads to flooding (as in Texas in May 2015), continuing rain storms pour water on saturated ground, with an effect larger than it might have been if the storm had not followed several others.

The Level of Risk

In the earthquake example, I did not calculate or consider a *single* potential consequence and its likelihood. I considered *five* – an earthquake that would have a limited effect, one that would have a moderate effect (with two possible impacts), and one that would have a severe effect (also two possible impacts).

But, there are more than five possibilities. There are hundreds. An interesting article by Shane Latchman[121], an expert on catastrophe modeling with AIR Worldwide, included this chart. It shows how there are many possible levels of impact – and each has a different likelihood.

---

[121] The article is at https://plus.maths.org/content/modelling-catastrophes.

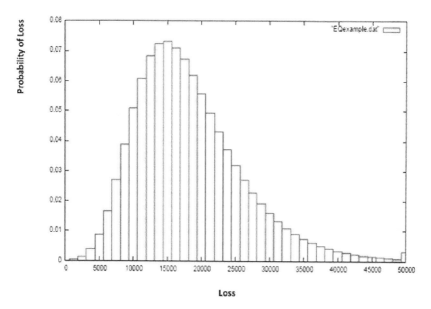

Statisticians know how to put a single value on this distribution (based on the area under the curve[122]). I didn't try; I just considered five points on the curve, which I believe were a sufficient representation of all the relevant possibilities for my purposes:

- Limited effect – 2 per year (i.e., 100% certain) with negligible effect.

- Moderate effect – 2% likelihood of a $100,000 effect and 10% of a $50,000 effect

- Severe effect – 1% likelihood of a $250,000 effect and <1% likelihood of a catastrophic effect

Does it make sense to pick just one of these and try to calculate a level of risk? I don't think so. Which one should we choose? I have seen people choose the greatest potential effect and others have chosen the most likely. These people then share a heat map with one point for the risk, when in fact there are five (in my example; there are hundreds in real life).

---

[122] When I was at the London School of Economics, one of the classes I took was commonly referred to as "Statistics for idiots". I have not progressed since.

The most widely-accepted way to calculate the level of risk is in the formula impact times the probability of that impact (P X I[123]). I have serious issues with that.

Should all of these be considered the same risk level?

- 1% likelihood of a $100,000 impact
- 10% likelihood of a $10,000 impact
- 20% likelihood of a $5,000 impact
- 50% likelihood of a $2,000 impact
- Near certainty of a $1,000 impact

Clearly the answer is 'no'. Advocates of a heat map will say that each of these is represented by a separate point in the chart of impact and likelihood. That makes a certain amount of sense.

But, in real life there are multiple possibilities and multiple P X I points on the chart (as shown in the chart above). How, then, should the overall level of risk be calculated?

The simple way is to take the sum of the calculated P X I for each possibility (in the earthquake example of five points, that is 2% X $100,000 + 10% X $50,000 + 1% X $250,000 + 0.5% X $5,000,000, which comes to $34,500). This may be simple, but it's not useful. Statisticians and modelers would use more sophisticated methods to calculate an overall level of risk.

But is a single, calculated level of risk a meaningful number? Can I compare it to some other number to determine whether it is a risk I should take?

In some situations, especially in financial services, calculating the overall levels of risk for different investments or trading opportunities may be useful[124]. But I am reluctant to do this when considering non-financial risks.

---

[123] There are more sophisticated formulae, but the P X I is the most commonly used.

[124] I am not an expert in financial services and financial risk management, so I will not comment on value-at-risk or beta calculations. In general terms, I understand that these methods may enable more informed decisions as to whether the risk/reward is positive and the investment should be made.

My view is that the possibilities should be assessed individually and in combination.

- Four of the five possibilities in my earthquake example may be acceptable levels of risk. I am willing to accept them because of my limited ability to influence either the impact or the likelihood of that impact – and because of the reward for living in Northern California. But, in the case of the potential $50,000 loss, I may decide to purchase additional insurance or install flexible water pipe connectors at low cost to reduce the potential for loss.

- I know some people who are not willing to accept even a 0.5% possibility of a catastrophic loss. While I recognize that the value of living in this area is high, justifying my taking the risk, they do not feel that way.

A single number for level of loss does not enable effective decision-making when one of the possibilities is unacceptable but the calculated overall level appears ok.

A more complex example is when there is the potential for (net) gain as well as (net) loss. Consider a situation where management is considering bringing a new product to market. Let's say that break-even will be achieved if sales reach 10,000 units in the first quarter and the likelihood of different outcomes is estimated as follows.

- 10% likelihood of 5,000 or fewer sales – net loss of $300,000 or more

- 25% likelihood of 5,000 to 10,000 sales – net loss of $100,000

- 20% likelihood of 10,000 sales – break-even

- 20% likelihood of 10,000 to 15,000 sales – net profit of $100,000

- 25% likelihood of more than 15,000 sales – net profit of $200,000 or more

You can use models (discussed below) to help calculate the likelihood of each of these results. Some (especially for financial risk) might use a model to put a single value on the range of potential consequences.

But, does it make sense for management to look at a single number[125] (+$15,000 if you take the sum of the P X I calculations) when deciding

147

whether to go ahead with the launch? I believe a world-class organization would make its decision by considering *all* the possibilities. Is management willing to take the risk of a $300,000 loss because of the potential for a $200,000 gain? Does it have the liquidity to sustain such a loss? Does the potential for reward justify taking the risk of a loss? That decision can only be made intelligently when all possible outcomes and their likelihood are understood.

By the way, 'traditional' risk management only considers the downside. That is not helping management make intelligent decisions, as is readily seen in this example.

Another problem with trying to put a single number on the level of risk is that the calculation of P X I ignores other attributes of the risk, such as the speed of onset, duration, and so on.

Finally, if we look at the currency rate risk example above, the rate – and therefore the likelihood of it being at a certain level at some point in the future – is constantly changing. The level of risk is fluctuating all the time, as are trends in the rate. (Volatility is not limited to financial risks; we have seen significant volatility in predictions for economic growth, the safety of different geographies, and so on.) A world-class organization recognizes this and re-assesses its exposure and options for addressing that currency rate exposure (both upside and downside) all the time, especially when it has to make a decision such as whether to hedge or move the currency.

World-class organizations understand that if they are to make intelligent decisions, all relevant information about a risk needs to be obtained in the analysis phase and considered in the risk evaluation phase. The level of risk is not a single number; it is the composite of all information necessary to make an intelligent decision about whether to accept the risk and, if not, what action to take.

---

[125] Martin Davies of Causal Capital has an interesting perspective. He says that "Risk practitioners who evaluate risk as a single number will miss the shape of uncertainty". A December 2014 post, http://causalcapital.blogspot.sg/2014/12/the-shape-of-risk.html, explains.

Risk Models

Models can be valuable if used well, but can lead management astray if used without the proper application of judgment.

World-class organizations use models (either developed in-house or by expert advisors) to help estimate the likelihood of future outcomes. For example, currency traders use sophisticated models that increase their ability to calculate the likelihood of rate increases or decreases. Financial services organizations use them in making decisions related to their trading and portfolio activities. Predictive analytics and related technologies (such as machine learning) can search large volumes of data, detect patterns and trends, and estimate with a high level of accuracy the likelihood of different outcomes of certain decisions. An example is IBM's Watson[126]. Watson is used in a growing number of situations, including the diagnosis and treatment of cancer. The oncologist provides Watson with information on a patient's symptoms. Watson compares that information with the records of hundreds of thousands of other patients before returning a diagnosis – along with its estimate of its accuracy. Watson can then continue to search the records of patients with the same diagnosis and predict, with a calculated confidence level, which treatment is most likely to be effective.

If used wisely, models can be very valuable. But they are only as reliable as the assumptions they are built on and the judgment of the people who use them.

In January 2009, Emanuel Derman and Paul Wilmott published the *Financial Modelers' Manifesto* on Paul Wilmott's blog[127]. (It is well worth reading.) Here are some excerpts:

> You can hardly find a better example of confusedly elegant modeling than models of CDOs[128]. The CDO research papers apply abstract

---

[126] http://www.ibm.com/smarterplanet/us/en/ibmwatson/

[127] http://www.wilmott.com/blogs/paul/index.cfm/2009/1/8/Financial-Modelers-Manifesto

[128] Collateralized Debt Obligations. *Investopedia*: "A structured financial product that pools together cash flow-generating assets and repackages this asset pool into discrete tranches that can be sold to investors. A collateralized debt obligation (CDO) is so-called because the pooled assets – such as mortgages, bonds and loans – are essentially debt obligations that serve as collateral for the

probability theory to the price co-movements of thousands of mortgages. The relationships between so many mortgages can be vastly complex. The modelers, having built up their fantastical theory, need to make it useable; they resort to sweeping under the model's rug all unknown dynamics; with the dirt ignored, all that's left is a single number, called the default correlation. From the sublime to the elegantly ridiculous: all uncertainty is reduced to a single parameter that, when entered into the model by a trader, produces a CDO value. This over-reliance on probability and statistics is a severe limitation. Statistics is shallow description, quite unlike the deeper cause and effect of physics, and can't easily capture the complex dynamics of default.

We do need models and mathematics – you cannot think about finance and economics without them – but one must never forget that models are not the world. Whenever we make a model of something involving human beings, we are trying to force the ugly stepsister's foot into Cinderella's pretty glass slipper. It doesn't fit without cutting off some essential parts. And in cutting off parts for the sake of beauty and precision, models inevitably mask the true risk rather than exposing it. The most important question about any financial model is how wrong it is likely to be, and how useful it is despite its assumptions. You must start with models and then overlay them with common sense and experience.

Building financial models is challenging and worthwhile: you need to combine the qualitative and the quantitative, imagination and observation, art and science, all in the service of finding approximate patterns in the behavior of markets and securities. The greatest danger is the age-old sin of idolatry. Financial markets are alive but a model, however beautiful, is an artifice. No matter how hard you try, you will not be able to breathe life into it. To confuse the model with the world is to embrace a future disaster driven by the belief that humans obey mathematical rules.

CDO. The tranches in a CDO vary substantially in their risk profile. The senior tranches are relatively safer because they have first priority on the collateral in the event of default. As a result, the senior tranches of a CDO generally have a higher credit rating and offer lower coupon rates than the junior tranches, which offer higher coupon rates to compensate for their higher default risk."

Some believe that the authors are overly negative and that models should not have been blamed, at least to the extent they were, for the problems facing many financial services organizations at the start of the Great Recession. However, problems existed; the users of models did not question underlying assumptions; common sense and judgment were not always applied; and, companies suffered as a result.

Derman and Wilmott shared, in the post, the *Modelers' Hippocratic Oath*:

- I will remember that I didn't make the world, and it doesn't satisfy my equations.

- Though I will use models boldly to estimate value, I will not be overly impressed by mathematics.

- I will never sacrifice reality for elegance without explaining why I have done so.

- Nor will I give the people who use my model false comfort about its accuracy. Instead, I will make explicit its assumptions and oversights.

- I understand that my work may have enormous effects on society and the economy, many of them beyond my comprehension.

Models can be extremely valuable for analyzing certain types of risk, but only if:

- Common sense and judgment are applied, rather than taking the results of the model as gospel truth

- Consideration is given to the possibility than one possible outcome might be unacceptable, even if considered unlikely (discussed further in the next chapter)

- Recognition is given to the fact that assumptions have been made, which may be incorrect, and

- The model is constantly tested

Multiple Potential Effects

So far, we have considered the range of possibilities for a single effect. But a situation, event, or decision can have multiple effects. Each has a different array of possible impacts and likelihood, they may not occur at the same time, and some may be positive while others are negative.

Does it make sense to offset effects when they are in different directions?

I dislike the idea of automatically offsetting potential positive and negative effects. Let's say one is 'valued' at +$2 million and the other at -$1.5 million. Does it always make sense to evaluate the risk based on the 'net' of $0.5 million? No. First, the likelihoods of each potential consequence are probably different and it is highly unlikely that there will ever be a +$0.5 million impact. They may also occur at different times (for example, reputation loss may lag safety or compliance hits). More importantly, if you only consider the 'net', you won't consider whether the potential for a $1.5 million loss is acceptable. On the other hand, when both effects are acceptable then netting them to determine whether the "reward justifies the risk" makes sense.

Moving on to adding the potential effects of a single situation, let's consider two potential events for an oil company that has annual revenue of $50 million: a refinery fire and an oil spill from an ocean-going tanker.

In the case of a refinery fire, potential effects may include:

- The loss of life of one or more employees or contractors, with lawsuits inevitable (Legal estimates they might amount to $5 million per person)

- The closure of the refinery for 3 months following the fire, with consequential loss of revenue estimated at $10 million

- $15 million in fire damage

- Air pollution requiring compensation to neighboring communities of $5 million

- $10 million reputation damage

- $5 million in fines by regulators

- Continuing business disruption due to a higher level of inspections, at a cost estimated as $200,000

An incident could lead to some, but not all of these consequences. Judgment and common sense has to be applied to determine not only the likelihood of any one of these potential effects, but also the likelihood of a *combination* of effects. Where it makes sense to aggregate several effects and the likelihood of those all occurring as a result of the same incident, a world-class organization will do so. The key, again, is to provide all the information necessary for an informed, intelligent decision as to whether the risk is acceptable.

On the other hand, an oil spill from an ocean-going tanker might have these effects:

- Pollution cleanup costs of $50 million

- Fines by regulators of $5 million

- Other litigation costs of $10 million

- $10 million reputation damage

In this example, it is highly likely that all effects will be realized and aggregation is probably appropriate and necessary.

It is essential to use judgment and common sense. When aggregation reflects what is likely to occur in the real world, and where it enables an informed, intelligent evaluation of the level of risk, then it makes sense.

> The key to the risk analysis step is that it needs to provide all the information you need before you can evaluate the risk, to determine whether it should be accepted or treated.

****

Most organizations and both ISO and COSO suggest that risks be labeled (such as "high", "medium", or "low" risks). While this may be somewhat useful, the fact that a risk is "high" doesn't mean somebody should be waving a red flag. What matters most is whether the level of risk is acceptable or not.

For example, SAP made a "bet the company" move when it not only invested millions into a new technology called in-memory computing, but mandated that all of its products would be moved, over time, to that technology platform. The potential for failure was huge, but the company's management, with the support of the board, decided that the risk had to be accepted if the company was to continue to thrive and dominate its market.

While paying attention to high risks is important, I believe it is more important to watch and take action when risks are outside acceptable levels. If you have accepted a risk, there is at least an implication that you don't intend to do more than rely on existing controls and monitor the risk. But, if you know that it is outside acceptable levels, action is called for.

Chapter 13: Risk evaluation, appetite, tolerance, and criteria

Risk Evaluation

Once all the necessary information has been obtained, a risk can be evaluated to determine whether it should be accepted. If not, then action should be taken to modify the risk.

Before looking at what the ISO standard and the COSO ERM Framework have to say, here's a story.

In 1992, I was with Tosco Corporation, a publicly-traded $2 billion U.S. domestic oil refining company[129]. It owned a large and complex refinery in Martinez, California that was at that time highly profitable. However, the refinery's financial performance was hugely dependent on the relative prices of the crude oil it purchased (its feedstock) and the refined products (gasoline, jet fuel, diesel, gases, and so on) it sold. The difference between the prices of its feedstock and its refined products is called the "spread". However, the spread was quite volatile: the refinery could be highly profitable for a number of years, but then slip into a period of losses before coming back to profitability. Over a span of years, the company was profitable but any single year could be a problem. During one extended period of losses, in the late 1980's, the company almost went bankrupt because it didn't have the liquidity to sustain the losses. By 1992, the company was back to profitability, but the share price was less than the current level of earnings warranted because the market took the volatility of earnings into account.

In 1993, Tosco's CEO, Tom O'Malley, and the board agreed to purchase a large refinery in New Jersey[130]. There were several reasons for this, but the CFO[131] told me that the primary one was that while the spread for an

---

[129] It also owned and operated a phosphate fertilizer mining company in Florida, which it soon sold.

[130] The Bayway refinery, in Linden, New Jersey was acquired by Tosco from Exxon in 1993. It had been operated at a loss by Exxon, primarily because its production was surplus to its internal needs so the refinery had not been running at full capacity.

[131] Jefferson (Jay) Allen, a brilliant and highly effective CFO.

East coast refinery was also volatile, it tended to be counter-cyclical to the spread on the West Coast. In other words, when the spread narrowed or became negative (considering the cost of operations) on the West Coast, it usually widened and became more positive on the East Coast[132].

The analysts welcomed the news that the volatility of the company's earnings would be reduced and more certainty created, and the share price rose far more than would be justified based simply on the enlarged company's revenue or earnings.

When the board and executive management considered strategic options, they considered not only the likelihood that earnings could fail to achieve targets, but the volatility of the earnings. Volatility was an attribute of the risk that was important to them, in addition to likelihood and impact.

Over the years, Tosco grew substantially. By 2000, it had eight refineries in Northern and Southern California, New Jersey, Pennsylvania, Louisiana, Illinois, and Washington. They were 'at risk' from natural disasters, including earthquakes, hurricanes, and tornados (not to mention tsunamis and floods). The likelihood of a $100 million loss from one of these hitting one of the refineries might be about the same. But there is one significant difference between earthquake, hurricane, and tornado-related risks.

An earthquake comes with no warning. One second everything is calm, the next everything is rattling. But, with a tornado there is usually some degree of warning, and with a hurricane the alert goes out hours or even days in advance of it hitting.

This concept is referred to as "risk velocity". If you have more time to respond to a potential event, then you may be more able to accept the possibility of that event.

A similar idea relates to the speed at which you can obtain information about a risk. Dr. Keith Smith[133] calls this Risk Clockspeed. He coined the

---

[132] The nature of the U.S. market, due to the vast distances between the East and West coasts, and because the sources of supply of crude oil tended to be different (Alaska and California crude plus some South American crude on the West Coast, and Middle Eastern and North Atlantic crude on the West coast), meant that demand for refined products in the West was rarely met by refineries outside the region, and the same went for demand in the East.

[133] Keith Smith is an English risk management consultant with RiskCovered and a non-executive director of the Institute of Risk Management.

term in 2006 and he defines it as "The rate at which the information necessary to understand and manage a risk becomes available." The idea is that the faster you have quality information, the sooner you can make a quality response.

What I am working towards is that when you evaluate a risk, you often need to consider more than the array of potential impacts and the likelihood of those impacts. Often, other attributes of the risk need to be considered.

Sometimes, more information is needed than is available when a decision-maker needs to evaluate a risk. In that case, which I believe is often the case when a new risk emerges, it is necessary to return momentarily to the risk analysis step[134].

Risk Appetite and Tolerance

Evaluating a risk to determine whether it is acceptable or not requires what ISO refers to as 'risk criteria' and COSO refers to as a combination of 'risk appetite' and 'risk tolerance'.

I am not a big fan of 'risk appetite', not because it is necessarily wrong in theory, but because the practice seems massively flawed.

This is how the COSO *Enterprise Risk Management – Integrated Framework* defines risk appetite.

> Risk appetite is the amount of risk, on a broad level, an organization is willing to accept in pursuit of value. Each organization pursues various objectives to add value and should broadly understand the risk it is willing to undertake in doing so.

---

[134] Both ISO and COSO assume that the criteria against which you evaluate a risk can be defined before the risk is analyzed let alone evaluated. I don't believe that is always true. While you may be able to define a "scale" for describing risk levels, you can't always predict what are acceptable levels of risk – because conditions change, and because every risk should be evaluated with consideration of the potential for reward (i.e., "it's worth taking the risk"), the options and their cost for taking action, and so on.

One of the immediate problems is that it talks about an "amount of risk". As we have seen, there are more often than not multiple potential impacts from a possible situation, event, or decision and each of those potential impacts has a different likelihood. When people look at the COSO definition, they see risk appetite as a single number or value. They may say that their risk appetite is $100 million. Others prefer to use descriptive language, such as "The organization has a higher risk appetite related to strategic objectives and is willing to accept higher losses in the pursuit of higher returns."

Whether in life or business, people make decisions to take a risk because of the *likelihood* of potential impacts – not the size of the impact alone. Rather than the risk appetite being $100 million, it is the 5% (say) likelihood of a $100 million impact.

Setting that critical objection aside for the moment, it is downright silly (and I make no apology for saying this) to put a single value on the level of risk that an organization is willing to accept in the pursuit of value. COSO may talk about "the amount of risk, on a broad level", implying that there is a single number, but I don't believe that the authors of the COSO Framework meant that you can aggregate *all* your different risks into a single number.

Every organization has multiple types of risk, from compliance (the risk of not complying with laws and regulations) to employee safety, financial loss, reputation damage, loss of customers, inability to protect intellectual property, and so on. How can you add each of these up and arrive at a total that is meaningful – even if you could put a number on each of the risks individually?

If a company sets its risk appetite at $10 million, then that might be the total of these different forms of risk:

Non-compliance with applicable laws and regulations	$1,000,000
Loss in value of foreign currency due to exchange rate changes	$1,500,000
Quality in manufacturing leading to customer issues	$2,000,000
Employee safety	$1,500,000

Loss of intellectual property	$1,000,000
Competitor-driven price pressure affecting revenue	$2,000,000
Other	$1,000,000

The first and important observation is that no company should, for many reasons including legal ones, consider putting a number on the level of acceptable employee safety issues; the closest I might consider is the number of lost days, but that is not a good measure of the impact of an employee safety event and might also be considered as indicating a lack of appropriate concern for the safety of employees (and others). Putting zero as the level of risk is also absurd, because the only way to eliminate the potential for a safety incident is to shut down.

I have another important problem in that I want to manage each of these in isolation. For example, I want to make sure that I am not taking an unacceptable level of risk of non-compliance with applicable laws and regulations *irrespective* of what is happening to other risks. In fact, I want to make sure I am not taking an unacceptable level of risk of non-compliance with *each* law and regulation that is applicable. Does it make sense to aggregate the risk of non-compliance with environmental regulations, safety standards, financial reporting rules, corruption and bribery provisions, and so on? No. Each of these should be managed individually.

When you start aggregating risks into a single number and base decisions on acceptable levels of risk on that total, it implies (using the example above) that if the level of quality risk drops from $2m to $1.5m but my risk appetite remains at $10m, I can accept an increase in the risk of non-compliance from $1m to $1.5m. That is absurd.

The other form of expression of risk appetite is the descriptive form. The example I gave earlier was "The organization has a higher risk appetite related to strategic objectives and is willing to accept higher losses in the pursuit of higher returns." Does this mean anything? Will it guide a decision-maker when he considering how much risk is acceptable? No.

Saying that "The organization has a higher risk appetite related to strategic objectives and is willing to accept higher losses in the pursuit of higher returns", or "The organization has a low risk appetite related to

159

risky ventures and, therefore, is willing to invest in new business but with a low appetite for potential losses" may make the executive team feel good, believe they have 'ticked the risk appetite box', but it accomplishes absolutely nothing at all.

Both of these examples of risk appetite statements were taken from a report commissioned[135] and published by COSO in 2012: *Enterprise Risk Management — Understanding and Communicating Risk Appetite*. The publication does, however, make some useful points that merit our consideration. For example, it makes it clear that the consideration of risk and what is an acceptable level of risk should be part of strategy-setting and decision-making.

> As an organization decides on its objectives and its approach to achieving strategic goals, it should consider the risks involved, and its appetite for such risks, as a basis for making those important decisions. Those in governance roles should explicitly understand risk appetite when defining and pursuing objectives, formulating strategy, and allocating resources. The board should also consider risk appetite when it approves management actions, especially budgets, strategic plans, and new products, services, or markets (in other words, a business case).

The COSO publication also gets it right when it says that the people taking risk, and that includes every decision-maker, need to know what level of risk is acceptable to the board and top management. It says:

> To effectively adopt risk appetite, an organization must take three key steps:
>
> 1. Management develops, with board review and concurrence, a view of the organization's overall risk appetite.
>
> 2. This view of risk appetite is translated into a written or oral form that can be shared across the organization.
>
> 3. Management monitors the risk appetite over time, adjusting how it is expressed as business and operational conditions warrant,

---

[135] The authors are Professor Larry Rittenberg and Frank Martens of PwC

This is critical and correct: "Risk appetite should be descriptive enough to guide actions across the organization".

However, while I agree that the board and top management need to know whether risk is being taken at a level that is desirable, the idea that this can be done with a single number is beyond my comprehension.

First, those risks that should be managed individually should not be lumped together.

Secondly and as I said before, an acceptable level of risk is not limited to the impact – it should *always* include the likelihood of the impact and may include other criteria as well. For example, let's look again at that challenge I posted on my blog. I asked which of these three strategies should be selected:

a.   A 20% likelihood of a $50 loss and a 50% likelihood of a $50 gain

b.   A 30% likelihood of a $50 loss and a 10% likelihood of a $500 gain

c.   A 10% likelihood of a $50 loss and a 90% likelihood of a $10 gain

Some people 'value' each option using P X I. They would value option (a) as 0.5 X $50 - 0.2 X $50, giving a value of $15. Option (b) is $35, and option (c) is $4.

In each case, the potential loss, if things go poorly, is $50. What is important is whether you can afford to lose $50 at all. Is a 10%, 20%, or 30% possibility of losing $50 acceptable? Are you willing to accept a higher likelihood of a loss for the opportunity to realize a larger gain?

Then there is the issue, discussed earlier, that most situations have multiple potential consequences, each with a different likelihood. A single number is not the way to assess risk when there is an array of possible outcomes.

There simply is no easy answer. Judgment is called for. But, in order to exercise informed judgment, all the relevant information about the risk, including both the potential for loss and the potential for reward, and possibly other criteria, must be available.

COSO tries to get around the issue that a "broad level" risk appetite statement creates – not being useful to individual decision-makers – with "risk tolerance". Some confuse risk appetite and tolerance, even using the terms interchangeably, but COSO sees them as different and complementary.

This is how risk tolerance is explained in *Enterprise Risk Management — Understanding and Communicating Risk Appetite.*

> Risk tolerance relates to risk appetite but differs in one fundamental way: risk tolerance represents the application of risk appetite to specific objectives. Risk tolerance is defined [in the COSO Framework] as:
>
>> "The acceptable level of variation relative to achievement of a specific objective", and often is best measured in the same units as those used to measure the related objective.
>
> In setting risk tolerance, management considers the relative importance of the related objective and aligns risk tolerances with risk appetite. Operating within risk tolerances helps ensure that the entity remains within its risk appetite and, in turn, that the entity will achieve its objectives.

So, risk tolerance is an "acceptable level of variation". They use an example like this: the target revenue is $75m, but the company is willing to accept $70m. The logic of this example escapes me: if the company is willing to accept a $5m variation from the $75m target to $70m, then their true target is $70m. Also, perhaps they would accept a 5% possibility of $70m, but not a 35% possibility.

Frankly, I would prefer that COSO talk about risk tolerance as (my definition) "an acceptable likelihood of a defined level of variation".

Fortunately, the examples of risk tolerance statements in *Enterprise Risk Management — Understanding and Communicating Risk Appetite* make more sense. But first, let's examine more of what they have to say about risk appetite and tolerance.

> While risk appetite is broad, risk tolerance is tactical and operational. Risk tolerance must be expressed in such a way that it can be
>
> - mapped into the same metrics the organization uses to measure success;
> - applied to all four categories of objectives (strategic, operations, reporting, and compliance); and

- implemented by operational personnel throughout the organization.

  Because risk tolerance is defined within the context of objectives and risk appetite, it should be communicated using the metrics in place to measure performance. In that way, risk tolerance sets the boundaries of acceptable performance variability.

Again, COSO is talking in terms of acceptable consequences when they should be talking about the acceptable level *likelihood* of a specific consequence (or array of consequences and their likelihoods).

But, as I said, they do have some examples of risk tolerance statements that I find acceptable. They include:

> While we expect a return of 18% on this investment, we are not willing to take more than a 25% chance that the investment leads to a loss of more than 50% of our existing capital.

> We will not accept more than a 5% risk that a new line of business will reduce our operating earnings by more than 5% over the next ten years.

> We strive to treat all emergency room patients within two hours and critically ill patients within 15 minutes. However, management accepts that in rare situations (5% of the time) patients in need of non-life-threatening attention may not receive that attention for up to four hours.

The trouble is that you can't roll these up to an aggregate level of risk across the organization.

What you may be able to do is establish multiple risk appetites, one for each of the risks that you want to manage at an individual level, and only combine different risks when it makes sense to do so. For example, it may make sense to aggregate the risk of not achieving revenue targets due to (a) the loss of a key customer in China; (b) the failure of the expansion into Russia; and (c) the loss of key sales personnel in Germany. While none of these risks may rise to the level that their effect on revenue means that earnings targets are not met, there is a real possibility that should more than one of the risks materialize, the earnings target may not be met.

In other words, when it makes sense to manage a risk at an aggregated level, we should do so. But when it makes better sense to manage it at an individual level, then that is where acceptable levels should be defined.

I agree with the following statement in the publication.

To be effective, risk appetite must be

- operationalized through appropriate risk tolerances;

- stated in a way that assists management in decision making; and

- specific enough to be monitored by management and others responsible for risk management.

As Jim DeLoach of Protiviti says in *Defining Risk Appetite*[136], "For the risk appetite statement to work, it must be actionable by management; that is, it must influence organizational behavior and have a meaningful impact on the company's execution of its business strategy". Unfortunately, I do not believe that risk appetite and tolerance, as presented by COSO, come close to achieving this objective.

While establishing broad level risk appetite statements helps management and the board discuss, set, and then know when aggregate levels of risk exceed acceptable levels, they fail to guide decision-makers at all levels across the organization when they make the decisions that change the level of risk.

Who are these decision-makers? When COSO talks about risk appetite, it focuses on the CEO and his executive team and the strategic decisions they are making. While risk appetite may be an effective tool for discussing the risks that the board is comfortable having the CEO take or manage at a strategic level, risk is actually taken every day by decision-makers at all levels across the organization. Decision-makers include:

- Procurement officers determining which vendors to select and the quantity of product to order

- Manufacturing quality control personnel when deciding whether to accept a production batch

---

[136] One of Protiviti's *Early Mover Series: Integrating Corporate Performance Management and Risk Management*, 2012

- Credit personnel deciding whether to grant a new customer credit, and at what level

- Managers deciding whether and how to discipline problem employees

- Human Resource managers deciding whether to present a candidate for employment

- Finance personnel performing flux reviews on a general ledger account, who have to decide whether to accept or to ask for additional explanation for trends or unusual transactions

- … and many other first and second-level managers

Risk tolerance is intended to guide these decision-makers, from senior executives to procurement officers; but if you look at the three 'acceptable' risk tolerance statements I referenced above, they are not sufficiently granular to provide actionable guidance.

Risk Criteria

While consultants have tried to fill the gaps in the COSO explanation of risk tolerance, I don't see it as a useful approach.

Risk criteria works better for me, even if it's just because the language leaves the definition of how you evaluate risk more open. 'Risk tolerance' sounds like it refers to a number, just as COSO defines it. 'Risk criteria' sounds broader.

Risk criteria can include, in addition to potential impacts and the likelihood of those impacts, the duration of the effect, the speed of onset, the organization's capacity to absorb the impact, the speed of response, and more. In other words, risk criteria can and should include all relevant quantitative and qualitative factors relevant to the assessment of whether a risk should be taken. It is developed[137] by considering the potential outcomes of a decision and determining which outcome is acceptable and how acceptability will be determined (i.e., the measures or criteria).

---

[137] As explained in the Australia/New Zealand Handbook *HB436: Risk management guidelines; companion to AS/NZS ISO 31000:2009*

In all honesty, I see risk criteria delivering what the COSO authors wanted to achieve with risk tolerance.

Risk appetite is a great concept for board discussions and helps management and the board to monitor risk *after the fact*, after the risks have been taken. But, unless harnessed with granular risk criteria, meaningful to guide individual risk-takers before they take a risk, it is not sufficient for any organization striving for world-class performance.

Managing risk is more than correcting course after you have gone astray.

Managing risk helps you avoid the icebergs rather than recover after you hit them.

To avoid the icebergs, a world-class organization has granular risk criteria to guide decision-makers at all levels across the organization.

> **Key point**: Risk appetite is a great concept for board discussions and helps management and the board to monitor risk *after the fact*, after the risks have been taken. But, unless harnessed with granular risk criteria, meaningful to guide individual risk-takers before they take a risk, it is not sufficient for any organization striving for world-class performance.

Financial Stability Board Guidance

Before leaving the COSO concept of risk appetite, we should look at an important piece of 2013 guidance from the Financial Stability Board (FSB). The FSB published a Consultative Document[138], *Principles for an Effective Risk Appetite Framework*, which included some definitions:

Risk Appetite: The aggregate level and types of risk a firm is willing to assume within its risk capacity to achieve its strategic objectives and business plan.

Risk Appetite Statement: The articulation in written form of the aggregate level and types of risk that a firm is willing to accept in order to achieve its business objectives. It includes qualitative

---

[138] The Financial Stability Board's guidance is not authoritative, although their framework has apparently been "endorsed by G20 leaders". The FSB focuses on firms in the financial services sector and expects their guidance to influence regulators of those firms.

statements as well as quantitative measures expressed relative to earnings, capital, risk measures, liquidity and other relevant measures as appropriate. It should also address more difficult to quantify risks such as reputation and money laundering and financing of terrorism risks, as well as business ethics and conduct.

Risk Appetite Framework (RAF): The overall approach, including policies, processes, controls, and systems through which risk appetite is established, communicated, and monitored. It includes a risk appetite statement, risk limits, and an outline of the roles and responsibilities of those overseeing the implementation and monitoring of the RAF. The RAF should consider material risks to the firm, as well as to the firm's reputation vis-à-vis policyholders, depositors, investors and customers.

Their definition of risk appetite is subtly different from the COSO definition. While it also implies that there is a single "aggregate level of risk", it also recognizes the need to address different types of risk and brings into the discussion "risk capacity", which I will talk about later.

When you look at their definition of a risk appetite statement, I can see room to define different measures, with qualitative as well as quantitative measures for different risks.

The FSB's risk appetite framework seems similar to the ISO risk framework and I will not discuss it further – other than reflecting that the FSB requires internal audit (or another independent assessor) to provide the board and management with a formal assessment of its effectiveness.

The FSB has some useful text on "key elements of a risk appetite statement". They say it should:

a) be linked to the firm's short- and long-term strategic, capital and financial plans, as well as compensation programs;

b) establish the amount of risk the firm is prepared to accept in pursuit of its strategic objectives and business plan, taking into account the interests of its customers (e.g. depositors, policyholders) and shareholders as well as capital and other regulatory requirements;

c) determine for each material risk the maximum level of risk that the firm is willing to operate within, based on its risk appetite, risk capacity, and risk profile;

d) include quantitative measures that can be translated into risk limits applicable to business lines, legal entities and groups, which in turn can be aggregated and disaggregated to enable measurement of the risk profile against risk appetite and risk capacity;

e) include qualitative statements for risks that are not easy to measure, including reputational and financial consequences of poor management of conduct risks across retail and wholesale markets, and establish some form of boundaries or indicators to enable monitoring of these risks;

f) ensure that the strategy and risk limits of each business line and legal entity align with the firm-wide risk appetite statement as appropriate; and

g) be forward looking and subject to scenario and stress testing to ensure that the firm understands what events might push the firm outside its risk appetite and/or risk capacity.

This repeats much of what I have discussed above, with some additional concepts, such as stress testing, that are more applicable to banks than other organizations.

But there is one point that is worth thinking about: "(e) include quantitative[139] measures that can be translated into risk limits *applicable to business lines, legal entities and groups, which in turn can be aggregated and disaggregated to enable measurement of the risk profile against risk appetite and risk capacity*". In other words, it is necessary to find a way to translate the top-level measure of risk appetite into guidance for decision-makers at every level of the organization.

If you consider the manager of the credit function in the U.K. subsidiary of a global company, she has to decide whether to approve a contract that includes payment terms of 45 days when the standard terms are 30 days. She is being pressured by the U.K. division's general manager to agree, as

---

[139] While this point mentions "quantitative measures", in (f) FSB acknowledges that some risks cannot be quantified and qualitative measures are required.

the contract is expected to be highly profitable. How can she know whether extending the payment terms will take customer credit risk for the corporation as a whole over its risk appetite? She can only know if the organization has found a way to (as FSB says) disaggregate the top-level risk and give divisional credit managers the guidance they need to take the right risks.

But, this example exposes another problem with the whole concept of risk appetite and tolerance. Should the risk related to extended customer payment terms be taken because of the potential for high reward?

Do the board and executive management want a credit manager to make the same decision on a contract with extended payment terms when the potential reward is 5% profit as when the potential reward is 35%? I doubt it. Yet, most organizations don't seem to recognize the need to take more risk when there is a potential for greater reward. (This is made more complex when the decision to take a risk is made by a manager in a different part of the business to where the reward is obtained.)

Some tackle this problem by calculating the potential value of the deal. They take into account the likelihood of loss and the likelihood of gain.

But this is problematic as well! Perhaps the company's credit position is fragile or it is strapped for cash and cannot afford to extend payment terms, even for great reward.

Judgment is required, taking all the factors around a decision into account: the likelihood of a loss, and what the magnitude of the loss might be; the likelihood of a gain, and the magnitude of the gain; whether a loss would exceed acceptable levels for the division or the corporation; whether the gain might create other risks, such as pressure by regulators because of a perception that the company is misusing its market dominance, and so on.

Judgment brings us back to the science and practice of management.

Managers are paid to make decisions, preferably informed and intelligent decisions. They have been doing so before anybody started talking about 'risk management'.

In 1974, Peter Drucker wrote[140]:

---

[140] *Management: tasks, responsibilities, practices*

"The main goal of a management science must be to enable business to take the right risk. Indeed, it must be to enable business to take greater risks – by providing knowledge and understanding of alternative risks and alternative expectations; by identifying the resources and efforts needed for desired results against expectations, thereby providing means for early correction of wrong or inadequate decisions."

Neil Crockford saw things the same way when he wrote[141]:

"In short, all management is risk management"

If the risk management process, specifically the risk analysis step in the risk management process, provides decision-makers with the information they need to make intelligent and informed decisions, then it succeeds.

Guidelines and Common Sense

Over the last pages, I have been critical of the COSO concept – as it is practiced – of risk appetite and tolerance.

But, I do believe that the board and executive management need to be able to set levels outside of which they don't want the company to stray.

These high-level risk appetite statements should *only* be set for those risks that it makes sense to manage at a high level.

In addition, multiple and separate risk appetite statements need to be defined, as it doesn't make sense to aggregate all risks, or even all types of risk (such as compliance risk).

The risk appetite statements will not always, maybe not even in the majority of cases, be defined in quantitative terms. In many cases, the risk appetite will have to be described in qualitative terms – whatever it takes to explain to decision-makers sitting in offices from Tokyo to Tangiers what is expected from them.

I also believe that there is little point in defining high-level risk appetites unless you are able to monitor performance against them, with prompt

---

[141] *The Changing Face of Risk Management. Geneva Papers on Risk & Insurance - Issues & Practice,* 1976

reporting, escalation, and action when it becomes clear that some are deviating from the guidance.

Even though a high-level risk appetite has been established, this has to be "made real" to individual decision-makers. One way to accomplish this is to 'disaggregate' the high-level risk appetite statement into acceptable levels of risk at lower levels.

Consider the diagram below. The company has decided that it wants to manage total customer credit risk. It analyzed prior experience and industry standards in setting the expectation that the number of days outstanding for its accounts receivable should be managed to 35 days or less (from invoice date).

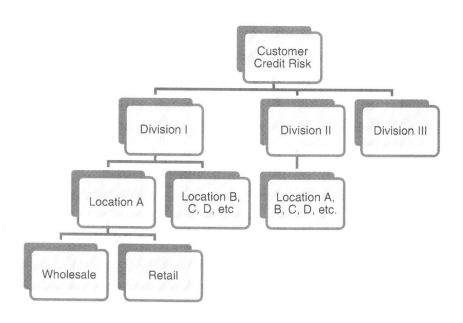

The company operates three divisions and has determined that the operations are sufficiently similar to set the same expectation for each: that they manage accounts receivable to 35 days outstanding or less.

However, the divisions operate in different geographies. In some parts of the world, 30 day terms are standard, but more lax payment terms are normal in others. Executive management allows the presidents of the divisions to set expectations for each geography that will allow them to compete in that market yet average 35 days outstanding for the division as a whole. In other words, contracts in one country may typically have 40 days if contracts in another are more restrictive (even resorting to requiring prepayment by customers with a poor credit history).

Division I in Location A serves two very different markets. Sales to the wholesale market may average 38 days while retail sales (because of the level of cash sales) average only 28.

Rather than expecting every part of the empire to work to a standard of 35 days, different guidelines are established for the different divisions, locations, and markets. Overall, these are expected to result in 35 days outstanding, and management monitors performance at each level to assure compliance with the local guidelines.

If the senior vice president responsible for Location C sees an opportunity to capture a major piece of the market by extending payment terms to a major customer, he uses his common sense. He takes the proposal to his management, who escalates to more senior management if necessary, so that an informed, intelligent business decision can be made.

There are times when it is prudent and appropriate to exceed the pre-defined risk appetite. Management needs to have a process that allows for exceptions to be considered by the appropriate level of management (and by the board if appropriate).

It is not always as easy to provide guidance to individual decision-makers as in the customer credit example above. In fact, a Deloitte study[142] in 2012 found that, according to a survey of 192 executives (not risk officers) "The main challenge [to effective risk management] was that people are unaware of what they need to do concerning risk".

> **Key point**: There are times when it is prudent and appropriate to exceed the pre-defined risk appetite. Management needs to have a process that allows for exceptions to be considered by the appropriate level of management (and by the board if appropriate).

---

[142] *Aftershock: Adjusting to the new world of risk management*

Consider a Human Resources executive whose personal and departmental objectives include staying within budget. When he is informed that the organization is going to expand its sales team into a new country, Panama, he has to decide whether to add staff in Panama, support it from existing locations in Mexico, or delay hiring until the next year. If he is lucky, he may be able to obtain additional funding so he can expand his department, but he will have to decide when and how to do so. Should he hire before the sales team is in place or after? Should he hire somebody in Mexico who can support Panama part-time? Should he hire an experienced individual who is familiar with the market but is more expensive, or 'take a chance' and move one of staff from Mexico as a development opportunity. His decisions are likely to affect the success of the Panama sales team; in turn, they will affect the likelihood that regional and enterprise revenue targets will be achieved.

The only way the Human Resources executive can have confidence that he is taking the right risk is if he involves all the other affected executives in the decision-making process. Multiple business objectives will be affected by his decision, and each is owned by a different member of the management team. A collaborative decision is necessary.

Frankly, I don't know how you can expect to have predefined guidance for an executive in this kind of situation.

When I was with Maxtor, I saw an exemplary example of risk management in our Singapore office.

The vice president responsible for procurement[143] needed to decide how the company was going to source a number of vital materials. He had received bids from about a dozen vendors, each of which had different prices, payment terms, manufacturing capacity, and performance history (including their history of on-time delivery, product quality, customer service, and so on). He had the option of selecting a single vendor (which would enable him to optimize his cost) or a number of vendors (allocating his purchases among them and spreading the risk that one might fail in some way).

---

[143] Maxtor operated two large manufacturing plants in Singapore and one in Suzhou, China. This vice president was responsible for procurement for all three.

This smart executive didn't make the decision by himself. He made it in collaboration with the senior vice president of manufacturing, the vice president of quality, the region's vice president of finance, and others.

While a risk appetite framework (as described by FSB) or a risk framework (as described by ISO 31000:2009) is useful, it is not the end of the story.

Today's business environment is dynamic, complex, and fast. Guidelines are part of the answer, but there will always be a need for managers to use common and business sense. All the information about a risk needs to be available and considered – with judgment – before an informed and intelligent decision can be made.

****

The ISO 31000:2009 global risk management standard doesn't talk about high-level risk appetite. It talks about *risk criteria*. As mentioned above, I like this term because it leaves open the possibility that more than the "level" of the risk (i.e., impact and likelihood of that impact) is evaluated to determine whether it is acceptable.

However, I am perfectly willing to accept the use of risk appetite, tolerance, attitude, or the phrase of your choice in guidance if:

- It enables the board and management to set expectations and boundaries for the risks it needs to manage (the board does not need to manage every risk, because that is an impossible volume)

- Management is able to monitor whether risk-taking is consistent with approved criteria

- Management and decision-makers across the organization are provided guidance so they know which risks to take; they know the consequences of their decisions on others as well as on the organization as a whole

- The guidance is sufficiently flexible to deal with exceptions, such as when the potential for reward justifies raising the acceptable level of risk

- The guidance is updated as business conditions change, and

- Common sense prevails

The last is the most important attribute of any guidance in a world-class organization. Risk management is an integral element in the art of management, and we should not chain decision-makers down to the extent that they are unable or unwilling (for fear of retribution) to take the risks that the board and executive management want them to take.

Risk Levels in a Dynamic World

Evaluating a risk against criteria set when business conditions were different is not a recipe for success. Risk criteria need to be updated frequently and challenged when they appear out of date or otherwise inconsistent with common sense.

Consider my old company, Tosco, and its willingness to extend payment terms to secure a major contract and accept the possibility that the customer might pay its bills late or not at all. In the mid-1980's, when I first encountered the company[144], Tosco was booming. I remember flying on one of its planes with company executives from its Santa Monica headquarters to the Tosco refinery in Bakersfield, California. The company owned and operated five refineries, each of which was highly profitable in an economy where demand for gasoline and other products was high. Tosco's capacity for customer credit risk was high because it could easily afford several customers to pay late because of its healthy cash flow and bank balances.

But the economy turned down sharply and so did Tosco's fortunes. By the late 1980's, the company was in deep trouble. Not only had it sold all its planes and all but one of its refineries, but many of those corporate executives had lost their jobs. The company was so cash poor that the Treasurer held cash meetings twice a day – to confirm they had sufficient cash to get them through to the next meeting! Tosco's capacity for customer credit risk was, essentially, zero. In fact, it offered customers huge discounts for prompt payment.

By the early 1990's, at which time it was under new management[145], Tosco was back on its feet. While it was profitable and had a healthy

---

[144] It was one of my clients at Coopers & Lybrand.
[145] I joined the company in 1990 as the head of internal audit following the acquisition of the majority of the company's shares by Tom O'Malley, who soon

balance sheet, I would say its appetite for customer credit risk was less adventurous than it had been in the heady mid-1980's and far more than it was in the gloomy late 1980's. The company was still concerned about cash, to the extent that it discounted some accounts to obtain early payment (a tactic justified by interest rates), but it was willing to offer standard industry terms to customers.

As the economy and the company's health turned, so did its willingness to accept customer credit risk in its pursuit of revenue. Guidance to its credit managers needed to change as often and as quickly as its health.

In 1992 or thereabouts, one of my audit managers (Laura Morton) was performing an audit of the Treasury function. She is a bright lady and when she saw that the company was making overnight investments of its cash at the end of each day in only the highest-rated U.S. government securities, she questioned the practice. She and I met with the Treasurer to discuss the situation. Laura explained that while the Treasury department was complying with the board-approved Investment Policy and investing only in top-rated securities, there was an opportunity to improve returns significantly by turning to only marginally less-highly rated securities. The Treasurer was at first reluctant to consider a change, but when we pointed out that the company was using the futures derivatives market to hedge its feedstock purchases and product sales (with a limited level of speculative trading that was closely monitored by the CEO), he acknowledged Laura's point. The use of derivatives indicated that the company was willing to take a higher level of financial risk, inconsistent with the risk criteria for overnight deposits in the Investment policy. The Treasurer discussed the matter with the CFO and they agreed to recommend a change in the Investment policy.

Sometimes, the company can be unchanged but have its willingness to accept certain levels of risk reshaped by outside forces. We saw this at Tosco in the late 1990's when a refinery near one of ours had a major fire and released thick smoke over much of the surrounding neighborhood. While we always had a low tolerance for air pollution risk, we knew that the community and regulators would be much less forgiving if we had a major problem as well. So, we doubled down on our precautions with special attention given to environmental compliance and related risks at board and executive meetings.

---

became CEO. Jay Allen was hired as CFO.

A world-class organization's management of risk is (as expressed by the ISO 31000:2009 principle) "dynamic, iterative, and responsive to change". This includes recognizing that there are times when a certain risk should be taken and times when it should not. A world-class organization has the wisdom to know the difference and acts accordingly.

A Personal Story

Let's close this chapter by looking at my 'earthquake-related risk'. In the last chapter, I analyzed the risk and now it is time to evaluate it.

Some people are not willing to accept any likelihood of an earthquake they would feel – even if the consequences are no more than a moment of shaking. Perhaps it's a fear of what they have seen on television or in a movie; perhaps it's a past experience when they were shaken up by an earthquake. For whatever reason, they will not live in a location known for its earthquakes[146].

I am not in this camp. I have lived in California for the last 35 years and am willing to accept a certain level of risk to obtain the rewards that come with living here: the weather, the way of life, and more.

Have I established a level of risk beyond which I would not go? I have not. I looked at the various likelihoods of an earthquake that would have a moderate to significant level of consequences for me and decided that they were acceptable. Sometimes, all you need to know is whether the level of risk is acceptable; you don't need to know how far from unacceptable it is.

My evaluation process included considering my options: if I didn't live here, where else would I live? There are few areas of the United States that offer the comfortable living that I have here, although I could certainly afford a much nicer home almost anywhere else (the cost of living here is among the highest in the world). Each of the areas I might consider comes with their own issues, including the threats of hurricanes, tornados, flooding, and so on.

---

[146] Curiously, some of the people live in areas (such as New England or the Mississippi Valley) where earthquakes also occur but many of the residents don't know about the risk.

So, I am willing to accept the level of risk I analyzed. But that doesn't mean that I don't continue to pay attention.

- Every time new information becomes available, I check to see if my risk level has changed. Sometimes a new fault line is detected and I have to look to see whether it is close enough to represent a change in my risk level.

- When I consider moving to a new home in the area, I look to see how close it is to fault lines or liquefaction[147] zones (an issue when I lived in Southern California), the history of earthquakes that impacted the area, and the cost of earthquake insurance and other earthquake protections (such as securing water heaters).

As I age, perhaps my willingness to accept earthquake-related risk will change. I doubt it, but will keep an open mind.

---

[147] In certain areas, especially where there is water or very loose soil, the earth takes on some of the qualities of a liquid during an earthquake. This has been a factor in some of the most significant levels of damage from an earthquake.

Chapter 14: Risk monitoring

At this point, we have identified, analyzed, and evaluated risks. But, we live in a dynamic world and these risks change[148] – and what constitutes an acceptable or desired level of risk also changes (or should change).

One high-performing manager for whom I have great respect made a significant mistake on a major capital project. The refinery he managed needed to build a new unit at a cost of several million dollars to take advantage of a market opportunity. However, there were options to how the unit could be designed. The new unit would create a number of refined products and each design would produce a different mix of volumes of those products. The refinery management team did an excellent job of looking at historical trends in the pricing and demand for the alternative products before selecting the option where the production mix would bring the greatest return based on anticipated feedstock and product prices.

Unfortunately, the market changed between when they settled on a design and when the unit was completed and ready to start operations. The management team had overlooked the need to continue to monitor market trends. Prices of the refined products the new unit produced had changed substantially. While the unit was marginally profitable, if they had changed to a different design it would have been substantially more so. If they had been alert, they could have seen the change coming in time to modify the design.

Risks[149] need to be monitored so that management can act promptly if and when the nature, potential impact, or likelihood of the risk goes outside acceptable levels.

Do all risks need to be monitored and does the monitoring have to be continuous? I think common sense and logic need to be applied.

---

[148] Both the risk source and its effect on objectives (risk) may change. We are primarily concerned with changes in risk, which can change without changes in the risk source (for example, by moving closer to a fire). But changes in a risk source may be more readily identified and they will typically lead to a change in risk itself.

[149] As noted, attention needs to be paid both to changes in the risk source and to changes in the potential effects arising from that source.

Our intuition tells us that the more significant risks to the organization's objectives are the prime ones to be monitored – and this may be the case for many organizations. But, focusing on the so-called high risks may be too simplistic an answer. For example, if a potentially high impact (adverse) risk has been accepted (perhaps as a cost of doing business, or because the potential for reward is a multiple of any potential adverse effect), is there a great deal of value in monitoring it? I think the answer is that it should be monitored only if it is likely to change in such a way that action by management will be needed. The change could be in the nature or scale of the potential effect, or in the likelihood of its occurrence.

A risk that has been assessed as "low impact" may need to be monitored if there is a reasonable likelihood that either the potential effect or the likelihood of that effect occurring might change such that prompt action is required.

The latter is especially important when the potential effect is positive – an opportunity for reward. The risk should be monitored so that it can be seized when appropriate.

But it is also important to monitor a "low risk" when there is a real possibility that either the potential effect or the likelihood of such an effect could increase to the extent that it becomes a "high risk" and exceed acceptable levels.

In other words, risks should be monitored if there is a reasonable possibility of a change that would require action. In addition:

- If the risk is assessed as not likely to change by a great deal, to the extent that it strays beyond desired boundaries and requires action by management, then monitoring can be less frequent.

- Monitoring can also be less frequent if the speed at which the risk might change is assessed as slow, providing sufficient time for management to respond. But if the risk is volatile in nature, and there is a high likelihood of the level of risk changing, then it should be monitored more frequently to provide management with time to respond.

- If it will take an extended period of time for management to respond to a risk breaching acceptable levels, then earlier warning and more frequent monitoring is probably justified.

To summarize, if the likelihood of the risk going outside acceptable levels is high, and the consequences of failing to put a response in place are significant, then more frequent monitoring of the risk is probably needed.

We are 'taking a risk[150], when we decide how much monitoring to perform and of which risks. That is the art of management and the decision should be informed and risk-intelligent with information about the extent and likelihood of the risk straying outside acceptable boundaries and the consequences if it does.

****

Risk monitoring is a responsibility of the risk owner and there are a number of tools and techniques for doing so.

While risk monitoring can be performed using precisely the same methods as for risk identification, I like the use of risk indicators (also referred to as Key Risk Indicators[151]).

While some rely primarily on historical records to project the likelihood of a future incident, 'leading risk indicators' provide greater insight. A simple illustrative example relates to employee safety risk; the concern is that an individual working at the facility would be injured or worse. It is useful to produce and monitor statistics of actual workplace injuries, paying particular attention to trends. However, it is often even more useful to look at what are called 'near-misses'. These are situations where an injury *almost* happened. Perhaps the worker was able to recover from a slip before hurting himself; perhaps a manager caught the employee just as he was about to do something wrong. Near-misses don't change the injury statistics, but if there is a change in the level of near-misses, the likelihood of a future injury is almost certainly changing.

Another example concerns information security. A small private company has no history of outsiders penetrating its security. A risk analysis based

---

[150] See chapter 18 for more on assessing risk management risk.
[151] *Enterprise Risk Management*, by Fraser and Simkins, has a chapter on *Identifying and Communicating Key Risk Indicators* (written by Susan Hwang) that is a valuable read.

on historical information would show a low risk level. However, if the frequency or level of sophistication of attacks is starting to increase, even if none have yet penetrated the company's defenses, it is clear that the likelihood that they will do so is increasing. In another scenario, the company might be involved in support of the local infrastructure (for example, maintaining a dam, power plant, or airport). Changes in the threat from foreign cyberwarfare units may be signaled by the federal government, indicating a change in the level of risk faced by the small company.

I like to follow these steps in designing my risk monitoring:

1: What is the risk that I want to monitor?

2: How often do I need to monitor it? How often is the risk level likely to change? How quickly do I need to know about the change in the risk because of the time it will take to respond?

3: What is the acceptable level for this risk? Do I monitor the risk against all risk criteria or just some?

4: How sensitive should the monitoring be? How close to exceeding acceptable levels is the risk? How much is the risk likely to move? By how much does it have to move before action will be required?

5: How will I know when the risk level has changed? What are the signals and how can I detect and interpret them?

6: What are the available tools and techniques for detecting and communicating the change in risk levels?

7: Who needs to know when the risk has changed and how should the information be communicated?

8: Are there other risks that I need to monitor at the same time? (So I can design a more efficient risk monitoring program.)

9: Now, I can select and then implement the risk monitoring.

10: But, I need to constantly revisit my analysis to ensure that change is not needed.

****

One source of information about the current level of risk is the internal audit department. They and other assurance providers assess the adequacy of the controls that management relies upon to manage risk at acceptable levels.

It is essential that the results of these audits and reviews are reflected in the assessment of risk. When an internal audit identifies that the controls are not performing as expected, the level of risk will almost certainly be higher than believed.

In most organizations, internal audit maintains the records of the control deficiencies they report and the status of corrective action.

I believe that a world-class organization captures the control deficiencies as part of its risk management system, reflecting the higher level of risk until the deficiencies are corrected.

This is discussed further, in chapter 17.

Chapter 15: Risk response

If the level of risk is evaluated as being outside acceptable levels, action should be taken by management. That is typically referred to as "risk response", "risk treatment", or "risk modification". I will use "risk response".

There's no real difference in my view in how COSO and ISO talk about risk response. The COSO language is fine:

> Risk response: having assessed relevant risks, management determines how it will respond. Responses include risk avoidance, reduction, sharing, and acceptance. In considering its response, management assesses the effect on risk likelihood and impact, as well as costs and benefits, selecting a response that brings residual risk within desired risk tolerances. Management identifies any opportunities that might be available, and takes an entity-wide, or portfolio, view of risk, determining whether overall residual risk is within the entity's risk appetite.

To convert this to my language, I would remove the word 'residual' and change 'risk tolerances' to risk criteria.

It is interesting to note that, in practice, multiple different actions may be selected in response to risk. For example, if the level of safety risk has risen to unacceptable levels, management may not only try to reduce the risk through training and increased monitoring, but may seek additional insurance.

One risk response that is rarely, if ever, mentioned is that the organization can change its objectives and strategies. This is one way of avoiding the risk and it provides the opportunity to take a step back and see if not only this objective (the one affected by the risk) but multiple objectives and related strategies should be changed.

For example, Maxtor designed, built, and sold disk drives to computer, phone, and other electronics manufacturers. One year, the CEO decided that the company's efforts to design a next-generation product were not only taking too long, but it didn't seem likely that Maxtor would be able to produce a product at a cost that would be competitive. The CEO led a review of the company's strategies, abandoned that product, and redeployed the resources to another product. Unfortunately, that second product suffered from several of the same problems as the first product, and the CEO and the board eventually had to change their objective one final time – to selling the company.

When an organization sets its strategic objectives, they may be interconnected. When the level of risk to one objective is outside acceptable boundaries, and it cannot be mitigated at an acceptable cost, then rather than dropping one objective, a world-class management team will sit back and consider whether other objectives should also be reconsidered.

****

Actions can be taken to change either the potential impact of a risk or its likelihood. Other actions may be able to change the duration of the effect, the volatility of the risk, and even the speed at which information about the risk is obtained. One or more of these changes may be required to bring the risk within acceptable criteria.

I say "potential impact... or its likelihood", but as explained earlier, there are very often several potential impacts, each with a different consequence.

Consider the chart below, which shows a range of potential consequences and their likelihood. The blue line shows the level of risk before actions are taken. One or more points on the curve may be unacceptable, and action is taken to change them. The actions reduce the likelihood of each of the adverse consequences, increase the likelihood that the effect will be neutral or slightly positive, but at the cost of reducing the likelihood of a significant gain.

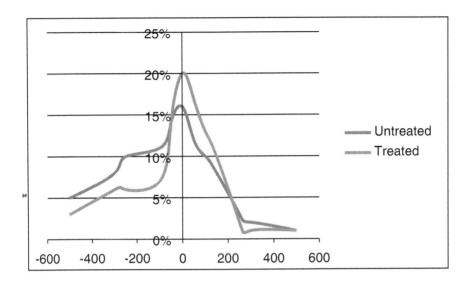

Some risk managers have a pre-disposition to acquire insurance to address and mitigate risk. This risk-sharing approach should, in my opinion, be the last option selected rather than the first. While insurance can cover, to an extent, the damage from an adverse incident, I would much prefer to limit the likelihood of that incident and its potential impact. Too often, there are 'knock-on' consequences to an adverse impact that an insurance policy may not be able to cover, such as the sustained loss of customers.

Management should use its common sense in selecting the response, considering the cost and benefit of each action and also bearing in mind that risk treatments very often create new risks or change existing ones.

However, this is a reactive process – understanding, analyzing, evaluating, and then responding to risk once it has been identified and assessed. I like the idea that an organization can *anticipate* a need to accept new or a higher level of risk, even before it appears. If management can build the *capacity* to manage risk before the need arises, it will be able to seize opportunities with alacrity and avoid possible losses while it implements mitigating controls.

Risk Capacity

Risk capacity is an interesting concept. In a 2010 article[152], Accenture suggested that "High performance requires a keen understanding of not only a company's appetite for risk but also its capacity to manage that risk effectively. Companies that walk that fine line between the two can better protect themselves and pursue new market-place opportunities."

Accenture went on to explain what they meant by risk capacity:

> It is a measure of a company's resiliency and agility—an estimate of its ability to take on new opportunities, as well as the scope and type of economic shocks it can bear without a serious decline in its operational effectiveness. Using a risk-bearing capacity analysis, companies can balance their appetite for risk taking against their ability to manage those risks. Neither too cautious nor too reckless, they can adjust either their capacity or their appetite to make more prudent—and ultimately successful—investment decisions. Risk-bearing capacity is multidimensional, comprising at least five components: financial strength, management capacity, competitive dynamics, operational flexibility and risk management systems. Effective risk-bearing capacity analysis can help companies establish stronger links between strategy and operational planning, which enables them to optimize capital allocation, identify additional resources available to seize opportunities, craft much more relevant and powerful performance metrics, and achieve better focus on performance reporting.

> Risk-bearing capacity also expands the traditional idea of risk management beyond financial resources, focusing a company on a broader picture of operations, management processes, systems, culture and leadership that can increase resiliency in the face of setbacks, and improve agility to pursue new opportunities. That is, it helps a company deal with both the downside and the upside of risk—to play defense as well as offense.

When Tosco Corp. acquired the Bayway refinery in Linden, New Jersey, in 1993, the CEO recognized an immense opportunity. Futures contracts for refined products in the U.S. defined the point of delivery as New York

---

[152] *It's all about balance, Outlook*, June 2010

harbor. The Bayway refinery was the only refinery on the New York Harbor so there was a natural opportunity to lock in the price the company would receive for its products by trading in the futures market. The price the company was paying for its crude feedstock could also be hedged with futures, essentially locking in the spread and gross profit margins.

The company already had a small commodities trading operation that handled its California refinery. The company moved that team to the East Coast and expanded it substantially – prior to the closing of the Bayway acquisition.

The CEO had built up the company's capacity to use derivatives trading to hedge a major portion of its crude purchases and product sales, and later the success of the Bayway acquisition was attributed, in major part, to the trading operation.

A few years later, the company was considering writing sales contracts in foreign currencies. Until that time, it had only contracted in U.S. dollars. Before it ventured into Euro and other currencies, it built a capability to hedge its foreign currency holdings and commitments.

Risk capacity affects your ability and therefore your desire to take risk to achieve reward. It changes the levels at which risk is acceptable. When organizations can anticipate a need to take on risk, by increasing its risk capacity it can ensure that it will be able to manage that risk and keep it within acceptable levels.

Risk capacity can be built in a number of ways. When Tosco set up a derivatives trading desk and then a currency hedging desk, it was building up its capacity to manage commodity price and currency-related risks. New technology is another way to enhance risk capacity.

Earlier, I talked about the need for the continuous management of risk. One of the greatest boons for the management of risk in recent years is the progress that has been made in analytics. Analytics technology has advanced in multiple dimensions, enabling the mass of data created by organizations, in social media, and elsewhere to be mined. The nuggets uncovered provide great insight into not only the current state of risk, but trends that indicate upcoming changes in risk. The new technology not only analyzes the billions of records available but can do so hundreds of thousands of times as fast.

For example, if you have a "semantic analysis" capability (which mines social media information), you have the ability to test a new idea or product and get customer feedback very quickly. A company can "take the risk" of introducing the new product knowing that they will learn quickly if it is failing and pull it back.

My final risk capacity example comes from the Accenture article. It describes how having a large amount of cash (or other source of liquidity), gives an organization the capability to take the risk of an acquisition. Arguably, the massive amounts of cash held by some of the technology companies has allowed them to make a number of acquisitions that were something of a gamble – because they could afford it if several failed. Similarly, some technology giants are willing to fund their developers' bright ideas knowing that while the majority will fail, a few will be a big success. They have the resources to absorb the small losses to give themselves the chance of a big gain.

Sharing Risk

As I said before, selecting a risk response is primarily a matter of common sense: identifying the options, evaluating them (considering their cost, any new risk they will introduce, and the likelihood that they will bring risk within acceptable levels), and selecting the best option.

One option that is often identified but has to be viewed with caution is 'sharing' the risk. Examples that are given include insurance and outsourcing. Neither necessarily reduces the risk to the extent that people may believe.

As I said earlier, relying on insurance to cover the damage from an adverse incident usually does not cover all the losses that may follow the incident. For example, customers may switch to a competitor; new product development may be delayed to the extent that opportunities are lost; and so on. In addition, the insurance company may not be able to pay the claims in full or they may dispute the claims. Payment may be held up for months or years, and may even be reduced because the company was at least partly at fault.

The risk that the insurer may not cover the claim is one that should be monitored closely. Several large companies have determined that the available insurance providers do not have the financial strength to cover potential losses. They have instead built the capability to self-insure.

Outsourcing a business service does not (except in rare cases) outsource the effect of a related failure on the organization. In fact, because the company's management is less aware of how well the risks from failures in outsourced operations are being managed, a strong argument can be made that the risk has increased. While it may be possible to sue the service provider in the event of a failure, that will have uncertain results and should be the last recourse. Instead, it is essential that management identify the risks should there be a failure in execution by an outsource partner; analyze and evaluate those risks; put measures in place to address the risks if they are outside acceptable levels; and continuously monitor the level of risk.

You only have to look at Levi's, Microsoft, and others who have outsourced manufacturing to a service provider in Asia to see how the treatment of those providers' employees affected the U.S. company.

Internal Controls

Controls are a response to risk. The reason you have internal controls[153] is to manage risk: if there is no risk, there is no need for the controls.

The ISO 31000:2009 global risk management standard spends very little time indeed talking about internal control, while the COSO *ERM – Integrated Framework* "encompasses internal control, forming a more robust conceptualization and tool for management".

The 2013 update of the COSO *Internal Control – Integrated Framework* has a section on Requirements for Effective Internal Control. While the great majority of consultants leap ahead to the requirements that the five components and relevant principles are present and functioning, and the components are working together, the overall requirement for effective internal control is stated as:

---

[153] Some, especially, risk practitioners, prefer to talk about "controls" instead of "internal control" or "the system of internal control". While I have some sympathy for this position (definitions of external control as the laws and regulations imposed from the outside on an organization), I prefer to use the more accepted term.

An effective system of internal control reduces, to an acceptable level, the risk of not achieving an objective relating to one, two, or all three categories[154].

When a risk is determined to be outside acceptable levels, it may be possible to add or strengthen controls to bring it within those boundaries.

One issue that I don't find many risk practitioners focused on is the possibility[155] that the controls they rely on to manage risk are not performing as they believe. These practitioners assume that the controls function as intended, but experience informs us that is not always the case.

World-class practitioners recognize the possibility that controls might fail. They work collaboratively with the internal audit team, re-assessing risk levels when control deficiencies are identified (as discussed at the end of the last chapter), and actively seeking internal audit assistance when they see the likelihood of control failures increasing. This practice is extended to all assurance providers, including the information security team; environmental, health, and safety functions; corporate security; loss investigations; corporate compliance; and others who monitor the health of controls.

Internal controls are the responsibility of management, who are also responsible for obtaining assurance that they are working effectively as intended. However, management frequently is unaware when controls are not being performed consistently, which is why the role of internal audit is critical.

The internal audit function should not only assess and provide a formal opinion to management and the board on the effectiveness of the risk management system, but also on the effectiveness of the controls relied upon to manage the more significant risks.

That does not remove the responsibility from management for ensuring internal controls are effective. Instead, internal audit provides a separate, objective assessment that should supplement management's own

---

[154] COSO Internal Control groups objectives into three categories: operations, reporting, and compliance.
[155] Some refer to this as control risk.

monitoring of the effectiveness of internal control (through supervision and other techniques).

The risk practitioner and management should welcome the assurance from internal audit that the controls they rely on are working effectively as intended, because otherwise the risk to the achievement of their objectives is very likely to be at unacceptable levels.

The monitoring of controls is discussed further in chapter 17.

Chapter 16: Risk management reporting

There is more to risk management reporting than the periodic reports that go to top management and the board. Each individual responsible for managing risk (i.e., every manager) needs current, reliable, timely, and useful information so he can do so – as an essential and integral element of being an effective manager.

Guidance tells us that every risk of significance should have an "owner". Who "owns" a risk?

In my view, the individual responsible for achieving an objective, at any level of the organization, is also responsible for managing risks related to the objective. That person owns the risk. The owner is responsible and accountable for monitoring risks and identifying when they are outside risk criteria, then determining the risk response and ensuring necessary actions are taken. (The owner cannot always take the actions himself. For example, the owner of a safety risk may request enhanced employee safety training, which has to be put in place by a training department and enforced by line management.)

That doesn't mean that the owner of a risk has authority over every decision or action that may change the level of the risk. As we have seen, the actions of one manager often affect risks and objectives in a totally different area of the organization. But, the owner of the risk should strive to be aware of how decisions made by another (secondary) manager can affect him and work to collaborate with that manager so that the overall needs of the organization are met.

For example, the CFO may be responsible for managing risk relating to currency fluctuations. But he will look to his Treasurer to perform any hedging activities, and his unit controllers to provide the Treasurer with the information he needs to address the risk. Similarly, the vice president, manufacturing, may be responsible for ensuring quality product and managing related risks. But, he will depend on his procurement, receiving, and quality control functions for many of the procedures and controls relied upon to manage those risks.

In many organizations, those secondary managers are focused on the achievement of their personal objectives and deliberately or through ignorance fail to understand that the achievement of an organization's objectives depends on their actions – specific actions that they may or not make, may not make at the right time, to which they may not dedicate an appropriate level of resources and management attention, and which they may not prioritize over personal objectives that drive their compensation or career.

This may be because the organization doesn't do a good job of identifying, using a top-down approach, what is needed, from whom, to achieve all of its objectives. For example, at a couple of my past employers, I was tasked with setting personal and team objectives and linking them back to one or more organizational objectives. This was a bottoms-up approach that failed miserably. My manager didn't tell me what she needed from me to achieve her objectives, her manager's objectives, or even how either her or her manager's goals were necessary to achieve the organization's objectives. So we all clothed our personal objectives in the colors of the organization's goals, without the faintest idea of what was actually required of us.

In a world-class organization, objectives (and related strategies) are set and cascaded down across the organization. Everybody should be informed and understand what is needed from them if the organization is to achieve its objectives.

****

Risk owners and those responsible for the oversight of the management of risk (on the board and in the executive ranks) need both periodic reports of risk status and alerts when significant changes are detected in the level of risk.

In chapter 5, on the value of periodic reporting, I said that I believe management and the board need two reports (in addition to a report on the effectiveness of risk management);

- The first is focused on objectives. It enables them to determine how well they are traveling the path to each of their objectives. It will answer the questions "is the level of risk for each of our critical objectives at desired levels?" and "do we need to take action to treat the risk, such as changing plans and strategies?"

- The second is focused on individual risks. This is especially useful when one risk may affect multiple objectives. The report will let them assess whether specific areas of concern, such as access to confidential information, are being managed appropriately.

Management at lower levels, such as of a functional area, business unit, manufacturing plant, and so on need similar reports. They are responsible for the achievement of objectives at their level, which should roll up to the enterprise-wide objectives. In the same way that they need periodic performance reports (financial and operational), they need reports that provide the information they need to manage risk.

A world-class organization integrates performance and risk reporting. As each manager views his performance metrics, the key indicators of progress towards his and the organization's objectives, he can see and take into account the condition of related risks. This allows him to adjust course, act to treat potential negative events, and prepare to seize opportunities.

Picture the dashboard of a car. It provides both performance and risk information to the car's executive (the driver). The information is continuously updated; the speedometer tells him whether he can go faster; the radio alerts him to accidents that may be ahead; and dangerous situations are highlighted by flashing lights. All of this is necessary if the executive is to drive safely and successfully to his destination.

Technology for Risk Reporting and More

When I was establishing risk management at Business Objects, my efforts were significantly limited by the lack of an automated system. My most immediate needs included:

- The ability for risk owners, those identifying, assessing, and monitoring risk, to easily record and share their assessments, and

- The ability to roll up individual risk information into reports for functional, divisional, and executive management and then to the board.

Priorities which would follow included the ability to automate risk monitoring (by integrating analytics and the risk management solution) and to support risk assessment workshops.

I initiated a project to acquire a risk management solution and was close to selecting a product when the company was acquired by SAP, which had its own risk management software. At SAP and other software companies, the risk management solution is bundled together with other software as a GRC solution. For example, many so-called GRC[156] solutions combine into one package functionality that supports:

- Risk management

- Compliance management

- Policy management

- Internal audit management, including the audit plan and audit workpapers

- and more

In the majority of cases, the risk management functionality is quite robust. But, I have a problem with the way companies go about acquiring a solution.

1. They may not be ready to acquire a risk management solution.

    The risk management solution is not software for the risk management department; it is software to enable the management of risk across the organization. There has to be a high level of management support for not only the purchase but then the deployment and use of the solution. That support should come first from the CEO and executive team, but also from the entire senior management team if lower levels of management are to accept and benefit from it.

    In addition, while a risk management solution may be an effective way to enforce consistency in risk language, processes, and reporting, it is better to have designed the basic processes and established how risk will be managed before selecting a tool to automate the processes.

---

[156] GRC stands for Governance, Risk management, and Compliance.

2. They don't necessarily need all the functionality offered by a GRC solution, but assess the options as if they did.

    More often than not, the greatest need is for technology to support risk management. Their need for internal audit management or policy management, for example, may be a much lower priority to the extent that there is no justifiable business case for acquiring software for that purpose alone. Yet, the choice of GRC solution (and thereby the choice of a solution for risk management) is swayed by the relative strengths of the options in supporting these less critical activities. All the users of all the functionalities, such as internal audit, vote and this can result in the selection of the second-best product for risk management because it is the better product for internal audit and policy management.

    In addition, many organizations rely on the assessments by software analysts (such as Forrester Research and Gartner) that judge solutions based on all the functionality the analysts deem vital, rather than the functionality critical to their own needs.

    When the business need is for a risk management solution, and other users of a GRC package are unable to justify the purchase of technology by themselves, the organization should base its selection on the effectiveness of the solution in supporting risk management. In fact, very often the organization should have considered software that only supports risk management.

3. Too few organizations recognize, when they select software, that they need to be able to (a) identify the risks relevant to each of their objectives and strategies, and (b) provide integrated performance and risk reports for each of them.

    The great majority of the GRC solutions have no integration between performance management and risk management. Even fewer have integrated strategy management (if they even have automated strategy and objective management) and risk management. As a result, they will need to build connectors after they have acquired the solution. This may be complex, expensive, and hard to maintain.

4. Not all of the current and future risk management needs are identified and considered in selecting the software.

Most organizations will include some basic risk management functionality, such as the maintenance of a risk register, the calculation of risk levels based on potential consequences and likelihood, the comparison of risk level and risk criteria, and the production of aggregated risk reports.

However, the functionality the organization will need to support it as it strives for mature and effective risk management is often not considered, such as:

- Automated risk monitoring, including the integration of analytics that needs continuous access to the enterprise financial and operational systems

- Scenario analysis, simulation, and cost benefit analysis (used in considering risk responses)

- The ability to considering a range of potential consequences and likelihoods for a risk rather than one potential effect and its likelihood (as I explained with the earthquake example)

- Support for risk assessment workshops

- Integration with the management of major projects, such as in IT, capital projects, and product development

- ...and so on

My personal belief is that an organization cannot have word-class risk management without one or more technology solutions. I say "one or more" because risk should, as said earlier, be integrated into pretty much every business process and not managed separately, in a silo. Different parts of the organization need different information to support their decisions and risk-taking, even if this is then captured and shared in a single enterprise-wide system.

****

In the chapter on periodic reporting, I said that every manager should receive the information they need to make decisions and manage risk. Different managers in different parts of the business need different types of information, at different frequencies, and in different forms. Some prefer a briefing and exception reporting, while others want to see all the detail.

A world-class organization will probably take full advantage of available technology to provide every manager with timely, integrated, performance and risk information. This will make them better decision-makers and managers of the enterprise.

Regulatory Reporting

The regulators in most countries require that information relating to the management of risk is included in reports filed with them. For example, in the U.S., the SEC requires companies with listed securities to disclose "in proxy and information statements" (such as the annual Form 10-K and quarterly Form 10-Q) the more significant risk factors that might affect the company's listed securities. Companies are also required to disclose:

- The relationship of a company's compensation policies and practices to risk management, and

- Board leadership structure and the board's role in risk oversight.

Decisions on what to disclose are management decisions, with advice from counsel and the risk officer. Consideration should be given to ensuring that all risks that are significant to the achievement of corporate objectives are included, although the wording of the SEC rules talks about risks that are "material" to the pricing of the company's securities.

In my experience, the risk officer provides input but the final decisions are made by executive management and the general counsel.

Chapter 17: Monitoring and review of the risk management system

In chapter 14, I covered risk monitoring. But there is also a need for periodic monitoring and review of the risk management system, including the processes, policies, and so on – and the controls relied on to manage risk.

Both ISO and COSO cover this topic, and I think the combination of their descriptions is better than either one individually. Looking at COSO first:

> Enterprise risk management is monitored – assessing the presence and functioning of its components over time. This is accomplished through ongoing monitoring activities, separate evaluations, or a combination of the two. Ongoing monitoring occurs in the normal course of management activities. The scope and frequency of separate evaluations will depend primarily on an assessment of risks[157] and the effectiveness of ongoing monitoring procedures. Enterprise risk management deficiencies are reported upstream, with serious matters reported to top management and the board.

From ISO 31000:

> **4.5 Monitoring and review of the framework**
>
> In order to ensure that risk management is effective and continues to support organizational performance, the organization should:
>
> - measure risk management performance against indicators, which are periodically reviewed for appropriateness;
>
> - periodically measure progress against, and deviation from, the risk management plan;

---

[157] COSO unfortunately confuses monitoring of individual risks, as discussed earlier, and the monitoring and review of the risk management system. When it talks about the "assessment of risks" affecting the frequency of monitoring, it is referring to the monitoring of the level of individual risks.

- periodically review whether the risk management framework, policy and plan are still appropriate, given the organizations' external and internal context;

- report on risk, progress with the risk management plan and how well the risk management policy is being followed; and

- review the effectiveness of the risk management framework.

The combination of the two tells us:

1. Changes in the business and the environment in which it operates (the internal and external context, in ISO terms) may mean that changes have to be made to the risk management system. As I said in principle #3, the management of risk should be "responsive to change".

   For example, different methods may be required to treat new risks; changes to the way in which the organization operates (including its objectives and strategies, organizational structure, and so on) may indicate that assessments and evaluations should be performed by different individuals or using different systems; or the criteria for evaluating risks may need to be updated to reflect changes in objectives, corporate performance, compliance requirements.

   Monitoring of the internal and external environments is required to identify when changes to the risk management system should be made. As indicated by COSO, that form of monitoring should be part of the regular management activity.

2. The effectiveness of the risk management system, including its processes, policies, and so on, needs to be assessed. As needed, upgrades should be made.

   World-class organizations will identify issues, such as the failure to perform risk evaluations promptly or delays in the identification of changes in risk levels, promptly. They will assess whether the issues were due to a defect in the risk management system, requiring corrective action, and take any such action immediately.

World-class organizations will also self-assess the effectiveness of risk management, including the level of risk management risk (see chapter 18), and take actions as needed.

Finally, as noted earlier, world-class organizations will have internal audit (typically) perform a formal assessment of the risk management system on an annual basis.

3. Internal controls will also be assessed, either through ongoing monitoring or through periodic evaluations. These are part of the risk management system, but audits and inspections (as noted earlier) may identify issues that require correction – even to the extent of making changes to the risk management processes, policies, and so on.

4. The results of the monitoring, review, and assessment of the risk management system should be shared with the executive management team and the board.

Chapter 18: Assessing risk management risk

This topic may appear strange. Risk management risk? Nobody talks about risk management risk: the risk of ineffective risk management.

They don't but they should.

Both ISO and COSO talk about *monitoring* the effectiveness of the risk management system. But they don't talk about *assessing the risk that it might not perform as desired*. That can be a huge risk to the organization. Executives and the board may believe that they have effective processes in place when they don't, with the result that they are making decisions based on imperfect risk information.

When you don't manage risk effectively, you are not optimizing longer-term performance. Decisions and actions necessary to deliver results may be poorly informed; the wrong risks might be taken.

I can make a strong argument that the greatest risk to the success of any organization is ineffective risk management: poor risk management means that the organization is likely to fail to identify and address both those situations that might cause it to miss its targets and those that offer an opportunity to excel.

Just as there is always a possibility that a business process such as customer billing or physical security might fail, so there is always a possibility that risks may not be identified, incorrectly analyzed or evaluated, a sub-optimal response selected, or the controls relied upon to ensure risk is at acceptable levels might fail.

Reasons for this include:

- Not every executive or board member embraces and embodies risk management

- Normal human bias when considering risk

- An unwillingness to accept reality

- A reluctance to recognize and seize an opportunity because of a fear of taking risk

- A reluctance to communicate changes in risk levels for fear of retribution

- Failures to detect subtle changes in the business environment
- Risk management processes running slower than the speed of risk
- Excessive centralization or red tape bureaucracy
- Insufficient, unreliable, or unclear information
- Changes in personnel
- The inability to adapt risk management methods as the business changes
- Competing attention for management time
- Decisions made in a rush
- The deliberate violation of risk guidance
- Failures of internal control
- Errors of judgment and simple mistakes
- ...and so on

Some of these are very interesting and worth discussing.

Embrace and Embody Risk Management

Perhaps the most common and, in some ways most insidious, is where executives and the board fail to consistently embrace and embody risk management. Often, they don't really understand how effective risk management enables better strategies, decisions, performance, and results. Perhaps they hear but don't believe the message. Either way, they pay lip service to risk management but make their decisions based on gut instinct (they call it executive judgment) without any disciplined consideration of risk and uncertainty.

Even when the board and the CEO embrace and embody risk management, there are often individuals in positions of authority that don't. Spotty risk management means that there are a number of areas of risk – risk that new or changed risks will not be identified, assessed, and treated – that put the success of the organization in jeopardy.

A world-class organization watches for this form of executive failure and acts when necessary to retrain the individual. Each senior executive from the CEO on down is alert to whether his direct reports properly consider risk when they make decisions and demand the same from their direct reports.

Human Bias

Human bias is one of the primary reasons risk management processes fail. While a risk is recognized, the individual leading the effort to analyze and evaluate it may have prior experiences that lead him to misjudge the level of risk (its potential impact, its likelihood, or both). "I've seen this before and it's nothing to worry about; let's focus on what is really important" or "Oh dear, the last time we faced this situation we nearly went under. We need to tell the board immediately!" Emotion interferes with a rational exercise and the ability to see and understand the reality of the situation facing the organization.

Human bias can also lead a manager to fail to pay the proper level of attention to risk-related information brought to him by a person he doesn't respect or by a system he distrusts. "Joe said that? Well, that doesn't mean much" or "The system is always giving us bad information" in contrast to "Mary said it's serious so we need to put our top people on it".

It is important not only for management to recognize this type of human bias risk but for each decision-maker to understand their own potential for bias.

Blindness to Reality

"There are none so blind as those who will not see."

"Hope is eternal."

People sometimes see what they want to see rather than the reality in front of their eyes. Wishful thinking is a real threat to effective risk management.

That doesn't mean that you should always see the worst in everything (which is as bad as always seeing the best), but that you need to make sure you are seeing things the way they truly are.

The willful failure to see things the way they are is a normal human trait, regardless of the nationality and background of the person involved.

It extends to a failure to believe that there really is a train coming towards you at the end of the tunnel, as well as a failure to believe that an offer by a vendor is as good as it sounds.

Both this failing and the potential for bias are risks to risk management effectiveness that not only should be acknowledged, but monitored to ensure that they don't occur with an unacceptable regularity.

World-class organizations have disciplined processes with measures that minimize human bias and blindness, such as second-level management reviews of all important decisions.

The Fear of Taking Risk

We all have natural inclinations when it comes to risk-taking. Some of us are cautious and risk-averse while others take risk eagerly, even when they have imperfect information. These personal tendencies influence how willing we are to take risks on behalf of our organization.

The Institute of Risk Management published *Risk culture: Under the Microscope Guidance for Boards*[158] in 2012. It says:

> Every individual comes to an organisation with their own personal perception of risk. People vary in all sorts of ways and this includes their predisposition towards risk. Personality research identifies two specific traits that contribute to this:
>
> - The extent to which people are either spontaneous and challenge convention or organised, systematic and compliant;
>
> - The extent to which people may be cautious, pessimistic and anxious, or optimistic, resilient and fearless.

---

[158] I made a minor contribution.

The paper recommends that organizations invest in periodic surveys and assessments that measure whether there is a preponderance of individuals who lean too far towards aggressive risk-taking or are overly risk-averse. While I recognize that there are tools for this purpose[159], I believe every manager should be alert to these tendencies in themselves, their staff, and their peers – and be prepared to have a conversation when such a tendency is seen to influence risk-taking that is inconsistent with the organization's risk criteria.

Variations in ethics can also adversely affect the integrity of risk-taking. Individuals with lower ethical standards are more likely to ignore firm guidance when it suits their interests. This is discussed in the IRM paper:

> Organisations need to pay attention to the ethical profile of those working in their business. Every individual comes with their own balance of moral values and these have great influence over the decisions they make on a day-to-day basis.

Even a world-class organization will hire and give authority to individuals whose behavior is inconsistent with the desires of the organization.

But a world-class organization recognizes that this is a risk, monitors its level, and acts when it is outside acceptable limits.

Fear of Retribution

A similar situation, human frailty, leads people to fail to communicate when they see that a risk is outside acceptable levels. When individuals believe they will be punished for being the bearer of bad news, news that their management doesn't want to hear, they may well hold back. (This is reportedly what happened at General Motors with respect to their ignition switch problems.)

Unfortunately, I have seen this quite a few times. A combination of excessive hope, a reluctance to face the truth, and a fear of what will happen to them led to project managers failing to signal that the level of risk to the success of their project had increased to unacceptable levels.

---

[159] The paper references the *Risk Type Compass*™

I can recall two instances where a direct report to the CEO succumbed to the temptation to keep information about significant areas of risk to himself.

Many years ago, when I was a vice president in IT at a savings and loan association[160], one of my responsibilities was contingency planning for our California data center. The executive vice president of the bank directed me to assume that any individual I needed for the recovery effort would be available where and when I needed them. This is an absolutely absurd idea, but my boss (a senior vice president) told me that the executive vice president didn't want the CEO to understand that a major regional disaster, such as an earthquake, might represent a risk to our business that was unacceptable and direct him to move the data center out of the earthquake zone.

More recently, I was leading the risk assessment of integrating an acquired business and moving it to new enterprise systems at an accelerated rate. The CFO directed me to assume that there were no risks relating to the finance organization. Again, this was an absurd notion but the CFO didn't want to reveal any potential issues in his organization to the CEO.

A world-class organization will make every effort to make it clear that individuals will not be punished for being the bearer of bad news. But, we are human and every organization has human employees who want to look good in front of their boss. As a result, they will be reluctant to pass on bad news and make it hard for their own people to tell them that "the emperor has no clothes". A world-class organization will monitor this risk (employee surveys can be illuminating) and act accordingly.

Changes in Risk Levels

It can be difficult to detect changes in the level of risk. Sometimes, the change starts small and grows without being noticed. Sometimes, the speed of the risk management process is slower than the speed of risk: the risk changed while we were not watching.

In chapter 11, when I was talking about risk identification, I said "Since risks change constantly, you need to be looking constantly". In chapter 14,

---

[160] Equivalent in size to a mid-size bank.

on risk monitoring, I said "Risks need to be monitored so that management can act promptly if and when the nature, potential impact, or likelihood of the risk goes outside acceptable levels". In an ideal world, management has the resources to look in every direction all the time. But ours is not an ideal world and we have limited resources.

As discussed earlier, in chapter 14, resources should be allocated to looking for new risks or changes in existing risks based on management's assessment of the possibility and extent that they will change.

Considerations should include:

- The speed at which the level of risk is likely to change. This may be based on past experience and there is always a possibility that management will still be surprised.

- The amount by which the risk is likely to change (its volatility) and how close the risk level is to acceptable levels.

- The potential impact on the business if the change in risk is not identified and an appropriate response put in place.

- The tools available to perform risk monitoring and the cost of doing so at different frequencies.

To quote myself from chapter 14, "We are 'taking a risk' when we decide how much monitoring to perform and of which risks. That is the art of management and the decision should be informed and risk-intelligent with information about the extent and likelihood of the risk straying outside acceptable boundaries and the consequences if it does."

But there is more to the speed of risk management processes. Not only does risk monitoring have to be as fast as the speed of risk, but so do the processes of analyzing, evaluating, and treating risk.

There is little point in identifying a change in risk if management only meets once a quarter to determine its new level, whether that level is acceptable, and decide whether and how to act.

Similarly, there is little point in identifying that the risk is outside acceptable levels if action is not taken promptly. If the decision is made to delay or defer action, that is essentially the same as accepting the risk for that period of time. This is one reason that internal auditors and other pay a lot of attention to the timely correction of control deficiencies, because if management takes 'its own sweet time' to fix the problem, it is in essence accepting the higher level of risk due to the control weakness.

The entire risk management process, from identification through treatment, has to be designed so that it operates at the speed of risk. If it is slower, then management needs to be aware that it is accepting the risk that new risks may emerge or existing risks change without timely treatment.

The Business Environment

An organization can be slow to respond to risk if its culture is that all decisions are made centrally, or if there is excessive red tape and bureaucracy.

Taking the centralization issue first, there are some organizations where the level of risk and how it will be treated have to be approved by a senior executive at headquarters. Not only can this slow everything down, but it injects the possibility that the human tendency of the executive overrides the insights of those closest to the operation. It can also increase employees' fear of retribution and so on.

I saw this when the CFO of one of the companies I worked for visited an overseas location. In a meeting with a number of employees, one individual asked him a question about an issue she saw (a risk to the organization) that he took as a challenge. His response was loud and aggressive, stifling not only that communication but further communication from that employee or any others who heard of the incident.

According to the newspapers, at least one risk officer in the U.K. lost his job when he informed his manager that the bank was exposed to higher than acceptable risk from sub-prime mortgages at the beginning of the great recession. The risk reports had to go through multiple layers of management before information was provided to the board, and the insights of the risk officer were not only suppressed but so was his job.

It is true that in some situations, the insights of those in the field don't paint the entire picture. A more senior executive may have a better view, and only after his perspective is obtained can reliable information be provided to decision-makers. The key is to strike a balance where the insights of those closest to the situation are considered as well as those who see the larger picture.

When the only way to report or communicate a change in risk is by filling out multiple forms, obtaining approvals from a series of managers, or buy-in where the culture is that everybody collaborates in decision-making, management of the organization tends to be slow. Certainly the management of risk is slow, but so is management in general.

This represents a significant risk to the dynamic management of risk, and through that the ability of the organization to respond to the potential for harm or opportunity.

A world-class organization seeks to find a balance in its culture so that changes in risk can be identified and addressed promptly. This may require thinking through ahead of time how the management team will learn and respond to new risks or changes in known risks.

The Quality of Information

Even if the risk management processes are running at the speed of risk, if the information they rely on is incomplete, inaccurate, old, or difficult to use, those processes may not be reliable.

When I worked at Solectron Corporation, each of the divisions and each of the regions within each division (and sometimes locations within each region) had their own, separate financial systems. When the CFO wanted to drive improvements in the levels of accounts receivable, it was very difficult to obtain an enterprise-wide view. The company had multiple accounts at each location with our major customers, often under different names (because many of the accounts were in the name of a local subsidiary). The CFO had little visibility and therefore limited ability to manage the total balance receivable from any of our key customers. The only way he was able to understand the amounts due from each customer was after a special project that took months to complete. That project had to rationalize the customer list (including determining which accounts belonged to which customer, due to the inconsistent naming of the accounts) before a spreadsheet could be built to aggregate the balances. By the time a report landed on the CFO's desk, it was already about 30 days old.

In 2013, I made a high-level presentation on risk management to a number of CFOs meeting at the Harvard Club in New York. I asked them what would happen if they stepped out of the meeting and called their office to obtain a current unrestricted cash and short-term investments position. How old would the information be? The answers ranged from the prior day's cash position to 30 days old information about short-term investment balances (some CFOs said the information they would want on unrestricted cash would be up to 30 days' old). When I asked how much of that cash was unrestricted and, together with readily convertible investments, could be used if the CEO wanted to purchase assets that had just come on the market, none of them knew with certainty what the current position was.

Any decision today by the CEO and CFO would be somewhat speculative, based on uncertain information about what they could afford.

Information is used at every step in the process of managing risk. If the information is buried in a report, it may not be noticed. If the information comes from an individual with little experience in the business, it is suspect.

A world-class organization assesses the risk that the information it uses in the management of risk is imperfect. Investments are made to upgrade the information where the risk justifies it; otherwise, the organization has to make the informed decision to accept the risk.

Changes in Personnel

Every time a manager leaves the organization, he takes with him an understanding of the business and its risks that takes time to replace. He also takes his knowledge of how the organization manages risk in its ordinary business processes and decisions, how it reports performance and risk to senior management and the board, and how it holds the owners of performance objectives responsible for managing related risks.

All of this takes time to replace, and there is a risk that the management of risk will not be performed as desired until the new manager is not only on board but up to speed.

According to reports, a major global bank had a trading operation in London whose operations nearly brought down the CEO. The senior executive responsible for the unit had to leave on an extended medical leave. She had been a very detailed supervisor of the trades made by the unit, but when she left the unit was essentially leaderless and supervision was high-level if at all. The unit made trades that, in hindsight, it should not have made and probably would not have made if she had been present.

Every organization has some level of turnover. A world-class organization understands the possibility and its effect and does what it can, what is reasonable, to minimize the likelihood of poor risk-taking by new employees – or by teams operating without a manager. Training and orientation of new managers is prompt and emphasizes policies, practices, and responsibilities for risk management. When people leave, and during the first months of a new employee, the second-level manager provides additional supervision and review.

The Ability to Adapt

I talked earlier about how risk management has to be 'dynamic, iterative, and responsive to change'. When the business, the environment in which it lives, the way in which the organization is run, or other factors change (including the nature of the risks that need to be managed), the risk management system must adapt.

Sometimes the organization is slow to adapt because of the investment required (for example, in new systems to monitor risk), but more often it doesn't adapt because the need to change is not recognized.

In fact, I believe the greatest resistance to change comes from the individual who designed and implemented the system in place!

It's relatively easy to know you have to make a change when something goes wrong, but a world-class organization recognizes the need to change and makes that change, even when everything seems to be going well.

Finding the Time

Everybody is busy. Everybody wants the time of the senior executives. Sometimes, it is hard to make time to think about the business, its strategies, and whether current performance and levels of risk are acceptable.

At Tosco, I used to spend a fair amount of my time traveling to the major locations and listening to the management team[161]. Every month or two, I would sit down with the president of our refining division, Dwight Wiggins. Dwight is a gracious gentleman with a fine pedigree for his position, having worked in senior executive positions at ExxonMobil before joining Tosco. We had some excellent discussions that focused less on the internal audit team I was leading and more on the challenges he faced running the major part of Tosco's business. For example, we would talk about his management team, relations with the workforce (and the unions who represented them), the impact of new regulations, changes in the business environment, the need to upgrade systems, and so on.

I learned a great deal from Dwight over the years, including his executive perspective on risk management.

One time, we talked about the more significant areas of risk facing the company, such as compliance with environmental laws and regulations, the safety and well-being of all who worked on our premises (a matter of great concern for Dwight), the volatility of crude and product prices, the cost of major maintenance projects (always tens of millions of dollars each year), information security threats, and more.

Dwight told me that when he was with ExxonMobil, the company performed an enterprise-wide risk assessment. Surprisingly, the top risk was not the potential for an incident such as the oil spill the company had in the Exxon Valdez disaster, or the failure of an oil pipeline such as they had when their pipeline under New York started leaking. The top risk, the only one they believed could cause the failure of the giant oil company, was a failure to properly blend jet fuel – a routine operation in any refinery! I saw immediately how a failure in the blending of the different

---

[161] I tell my team that I don't want them to go and talk to people; I want them to go and listen. If they are talking more than 40% of the time, they are not listening properly.

products needed to make jet fuel could cause that fuel to be deficient, with the potential for it to cause an airliner to crash into a major city.

The lesson I learned was to think top-down, what needs to go right as well as what could go wrong, from the perspective of what is critical to the organization.

At the end of one of our hour-long conversations, as Dwight walked me to the door to his office, I thanked him for his valuable time. "No, Norman", he said. "I should thank you! Our conversations are the only time I have to sit back and think about the business as a whole. I spend my whole day fighting fires and talking to people about specific issues. I value our discussions as an opportunity to consider the bigger picture."

Every manager has this problem – when can they find the time to think about the business and its risks.

A world-class organization has world-class managers who find the time to think – about the business, what lies ahead, and how to address those uncertainties.

Decisions made in a Rush

As a direct result of lack of time, people make decisions without due consideration of all relevant information, the options available, and the likelihood of the various consequences of their decision.

Every world-class organization provides training and encouragement for its decision-makers in the skills and techniques necessary if they are to be effective managers. That should include not only time management, but the need to be disciplined decision-makers.

When somebody makes a mistake, instead of blaming them for an error in judgment, managers should see this as a learning opportunity: an opportunity to help the decision-maker analyze his own decision process and where it might have failed.

Deliberate Violations

Unfortunately, in every organization there are going to be people who are willing to ignore the rules. The reasons can vary (perhaps I should say that the rationalizations vary):

- I didn't know. Nobody told me.

- I didn't think that rule applied in this situation.

- I thought you told me to ignore that rule, or that the policy was out of date.

- I needed to go ahead because the opportunity was so great.

- I didn't have time for this bureaucratic process; all of this red tape just gets in the way of running the business.

- Sorry. (The individual doesn't acknowledge that he thought the opportunity for personal advantage justified his breaking the rules.) I won't do it again.

While innocent mistakes happen, deliberate violation of the organization's mandated processes for managing risk – which should be seen as mandated processes for running the business – should be taken seriously. Disciplined performance sometimes needs a touch of discipline.

Failures of Internal Control

Internal controls help the organization manage risk. That is their purpose.

But the system of internal control only provides *reasonable assurance*. As the COSO *Internal Control – Integrated Framework*[162] says:

Effective internal control increases the likelihood of an entity achieving its objectives. However, the likelihood of achievement is affected by limitations inherent in all internal control systems, such as human error and the uncertainty inherent in judgment. Additionally, a system of internal control can be circumvented if people collude. Further, if management is able to override controls, the entire system may fail. In other words, even an effective system of internal control can experience a failure.

---

[162] Updated in 2013.

There is always a possibility that one or more controls may not be designed properly (to address the risk it is expected to help manage) or may not operate consistently as designed. This *control risk* means that the business risk is not at the level management believes it to be.

Management and risk practitioners in a world-class organization pay attention to the quality of internal control. They understand that controls will fail from time to time, if only because they are designed and operated by humans. The level of control risk is monitored (using information from internal audit and regulatory reviews, as well as from management's own monitoring of internal control) and management acts when the risk is at unacceptable levels. For example, attention is paid to the timely correction of control weaknesses identified through internal audits; in a world-class organization, deficiencies are addressed even before the formal audit report is issued.

Errors and Mistakes

Even a world-class risk management system is imperfect. Mistakes will happen; people will make the wrong choices. As with internal control, the management of risk is dependent upon people – and none of us are perfect.

But a world-class management team in a world-class organization will be alert to situations where the frequency and extent of mistakes starts to increase. Root cause analysis is performed to determine why the mistakes are being made: individuals making decisions without accurate information; people not taking the time for a disciplined process; and so on.

Organizations will not survive and thrive if they are afraid of making mistakes. Decision-makers are there to make decisions and run the business. Honest mistakes should not be punished while the reasons for frequent mistakes are investigated and addressed.

Chapter 19: World-class risk management

We have journeyed through the various steps in world-class risk management. How then should we describe it?

Is *world-class* risk management a step or more beyond simply reaching the highest level of a maturity model? I think it has to be, since 'world-class' must mean that the organization stands above and beyond all others.

This is my definition:

> World class-risk management is achieved when a prudent person would believe that all reasonable efforts have been made to identify, analyze, evaluate, and treat the risks to effective risk management. There is reasonable assurance that the risk management system delivers what the organization depends on for optimized outcomes, performance, and the surpassing of objectives.

Before I explain how I arrived at this definition, let's consider what ISO and COSO have to say. I believe this is important because the two have great influence – and are different from my view.

The ISO 31000:2009 global risk management standard lists what it asserts are the "key outcomes" of "*enhanced* risk management"[163].

1: The organization has a current, correct and comprehensive understanding of its risks.

2: The organization's risks are within its risk criteria.

I think using this list of outcomes as criteria for effective, let alone world-class risk management, is unrealistic for three primary reasons:

- We are talking about uncertainty and that means our knowledge is, by definition, imperfect. How can we know we have a "*correct*

---

[163] In Annex A to the standard, which is labeled as 'informative'.

understanding of risks"? How will we ever know whether our assessment of likelihood is 'correct'?

- Even world-class risk management is itself imperfect. Mistakes will happen. These "key outcomes" provide no room for human error.

- There will always be times when risks are not within criteria, if only because responses have not yet been completed.

So, I am not going to use the ISO outcomes as criteria.

How about COSO? The COSO Executive Summary says that risk management (a) "manages risk to be within its risk appetite", and (b) "provides reasonable assurance regarding the achievement of entity objectives".

I am going to discard (a) for the reasons I discarded the similar criterion from ISO. You can never know enough about the uncertainty between us and our objectives to be *certain* that risk is at acceptable levels, and there will always be times that risks are not within risk appetite, either because mistakes are made or risk responses are incomplete.

I much prefer the second COSO criterion. It uses the term "reasonable assurance", which is the right concept (as I will explain momentarily); but is it "reasonable assurance regarding the *achievement of entity objectives*"? Let's keep that thought and see what I wrote earlier.

In chapter 2, I said:

> I believe the effectiveness of risk management should be assessed based on whether it delivers the desired results – reliable, useful and timely information that enables better decisions.

I stand by this statement, but more needs to be said when it comes to distinguishing a world-class risk management system.

I suggested this definition of effective risk management:

> "The effective management of risk enables more informed decision-making, from the setting or modification of strategy to the decisions made every day across the extended enterprise. The processes and related policies, structures, and systems for identifying, analyzing, evaluating, and responding to risks are established by management

219

with oversight by the governing body to ensure that the effects of uncertainty (both positive and negative) on the achievement of objectives are understood and managed consistent with the desires of the governing body, for the purpose of achieving objectives, acting with integrity, and delivering optimal value to the organization's stakeholders."

Again, this is insufficient to distinguish *world-class* risk management from *very good* risk management.

I also suggested six principles for effective risk management:

1: Risk management enables management to make intelligent decisions when setting strategy, making decisions, and in the daily management of the organization. It provides reasonable assurance that performance will be optimized, objectives achieved, and desired levels of value delivered to stakeholders.

2: Risk management provides decision-makers with reliable, current, timely, and actionable information about the uncertainty that might affect the achievement of objectives.

3: Risk management is dynamic, iterative and responsive to change.

4: Risk management is systematic and structured.

5: Risk management is tailored to the needs of the organization and updated/upgraded as needed. This takes into account the culture of the organization, including how decisions are made, and the need to monitor the program itself and continually improve it.

6: Risk management takes human factors (that may present the possibility of failures to properly identify, analyze, evaluate or treat risks) into consideration and provides reasonable assurance they are overcome.

I believe that world-class risk management enables these principles to be achieved at outstanding levels, because (a) the organization embodies and embraces risk management thinking all the time, at all levels, across the organization, and (b) there is reasonable assurance that risks (both the extent and likelihood of failure) to effective risk management are at acceptable levels.

I will come back to that latter statement in a moment, but want first to address another misconception: that effective risk management, even world-class risk management, means that the organization has reasonable assurance of world-class *performance* and that *all* of its *objectives* will be achieved or surpassed. I think that is unrealistic for a couple of reasons.

1. Even with the most brilliant risk management system, the best management team and board in the world, surprises will happen. The assessment of global economic conditions may indicate a much higher likelihood of boom than bust, yet the bust happens. The likelihood of an earthquake occurring this year and disrupting the business may be 5%, but the earthquake hits 'against all odds'.

   Brilliant execution doesn't always mean brilliant results. Some situations are not only unpredictable but outside management control, so assessing risk management performance based on whether objectives were achieved or not is, in my opinion, misguided.

   While some may say that this is allowed for when COSO talks about "reasonable assurance", I think that risk management only sheds a reasonable level of light on *uncertainty*; it doesn't directly provide assurance on the *achievement of objectives*.

2. Even world-class risk management is imperfect. Mistakes will happen[164] and prevent the organization achieving its potential.

While I believe that organizations with effective risk management will be more successful over the long run, anything can happen in the short term. Companies with poor risk management can stumble, with luck, into the right strategies and make the right decisions. Yet companies with all the benefits of excellent management and processes may choose what turns out to be the wrong option.

So, if looking at actual results is not the best measure of world-class risk management, what is?

I believe that when you have the best risk management possible, designed to deliver the information you need to make intelligent and informed decisions, you should consider it world-class. Mistakes will still be made, but *the likelihood of the risk management system failing is minimized.*

---

[164] A world-class organization will recognize and respond to its mistakes.

The practice of risk management is imperfect, but the imperfections can be minimized by understanding and addressing risk management risks – the risks that affect the performance of risk management and its ability to enable informed, risk-intelligent decisions.

I said that when there is world-class risk management "there is *reasonable assurance* that risks to effective risk management are at acceptable levels". (Reasonable assurance is achieved when risk is at acceptable levels, and I use that phrase because we can never know for certain (as I said earlier) whether risks are at one level or not and therefore whether the risks are at acceptable levels.)

That brings me back to my definition:

> World class-risk management is achieved when a prudent person would believe that all reasonable efforts have been made to identify, analyze, evaluate, and treat the risks to effective risk management. There is reasonable assurance that the risk management system delivers what the organization depends on for optimized outcomes, performance, and the surpassing of objectives.

This is truly taking it up a notch from any risk management system I have seen or heard talk about.

When a management team and the board have confidence in their risk management system, they can drive the organization faster and trust in their ability to make sound decisions –leading to enhanced, long-term performance.

It may be controversial thinking, but I hope that it will stimulate discussion about what risk management really is, what we should all aspire to, and how it is an essential and integral element in effective management.

Chapter 20: Achieving World-Class Risk Management

Few if any organizations are world-class when it comes to the management of risk. As discussed earlier, while some are aware that they need to improve, others do not recognize the tremendous value that risk management can deliver.

Risk management is not just a compliance activity. It is essential for success.

So how should organizations go about getting from where they are to where they need to be? How can they achieve world-class?

I believe the first step is acknowledging that there is a need to change.

The need to change must be recognized not only by the CRO or other executive responsible for the risk management system, but by the CEO and the board. That is the only way to obtain not only the broad buy-in, but the time, attention, and other resources needed.

The second step is to know where you are. Many if not most organizations have not assessed their risk management program. A large percentage of those who have performed an evaluation only assessed compliance with policies and procedures, when they should have been evaluating whether the system provided those involved in setting strategies, managing performance, and making decisions with the information necessary for success – and the disciplined process for the consideration and treatment of risk.

Very few indeed understand where their risk management system is weak – where the potential for errors in the consideration of risk is likely to arise, the extent to which those errors might lead to failing to take the right amount of the right risk, and the likelihood of that happening – leading to failures to optimize outcomes and achieve organizational success.

Once the organization has recognized the critical need for risk management, and understands the limitations in its current set of policies, processes, and so on, the next step is to decide whether it wants to achieve world-class or not. Some may decide that they will be satisfied with achieving one of the top two levels in a risk maturity model. Once they have achieved that level, they can consider whether the value of upgrading all the way to world-class should be their next target.

At this point, management knows where it is and where it wants to go. As with any transformation or process improvement project, a disciplined project management approach should be taken. All the actions necessary to achieve the desired state should be included in a detailed project plan, with resources, timeframes, and so on. Status should be monitored by the executive team and the board, given the importance of this project.

The project management team should not forget to apply risk management techniques to the risk management upgrade project.

Once the desired state has been achieved, the work does not stop. As noted earlier, the system should be monitored and reviewed, risks to its effective performance assessed, and corrective actions taken as necessary.

But by then, the world-class management team will know how to apply world-class risk management techniques.

Acknowledgments

As I said earlier, I have sat at the feet and learned a great deal from many of the greats of risk management. I am particularly indebted to (in alphabetical order) Alex Dali, Martin Davies, Jim DeLoach, John Fraser, Felix Kloman, Grant Purdy, and Arnold Schanfield - all of whom were kind enough to share their valuable time by reviewing this book, correcting my inelegant or incorrect prose, and challenging my thought process and opinions.

My special thanks go to Grant Purdy for his continuing advice, his patience, and his contribution of a thoughtful and provocative foreword to this book.

I am also grateful to the executives and board members who were tolerant as I played at being an audit and risk executive. I say that I played at it, because it was rarely 'work' or 'a job'. It was always an opportunity to push boundaries and see how I and my team could better serve the organization. It was fun.

Finally, I want to thank the people with whom I was privileged to work – my team members and peers. I have had the joy of working alongside many exceptional people, who are too numerous to mention here.

And of course, I am grateful for the support of my wife, Diana, and my family and friends who have enriched my life and made this work possible.

About the Author

 **Norman Marks**, CPA, CRMA is a semi-retired chief audit executive and chief risk officer. He is a globally-recognized thought leader in the professions of risk management and internal auditing and remains an evangelist for "better run business", focusing on corporate governance, risk management, internal audit, enterprise performance, and the value of information. He is also a mentor to individuals and organizations around the world.

Norman has been honored as a Fellow of the Open Compliance and Ethics Group and an Honorary Fellow of the Institute of Risk Management for his contributions to risk management.

He is the author of three earlier books:

- *World-Class Internal Audit: Tales from my* Journey

- *Management's Guide to Sarbanes-Oxley Section 404: Maximize Value Within Your Organization* (described as "the best Sarbanes-Oxley 404 guide out there for management"), and

- *How Good is your GRC? Twelve Questions to Guide Executives, Boards, and Practitioners.*

Praise for Norman's last book, on world-class internal auditing, includes:

- "I thoroughly enjoyed Norman's book. My one regret is not buying it in hard copy, so I could tab it, highlight it, scribble in the margins, etc. It's the type of book I keep on my desk, available for quick reference or inspiration when the need arises. In his Introduction, Norman states his hope in writing World-Class Internal Audit is that it "...will amuse as well as provide some insights..." and that he wrote the book to "...stimulate some thinking..." I believe he succeeded on all three points.

    "World-Class Internal Audit is not a textbook or reference book containing audit programs or other details which can be used verbatim; there are many great resources available for this purpose. What I liked most about Norman's book is that the story of his personal career journey highly is relatable, despite being nothing like my own. He presents short stories about specific moments in his career with brutal introspection, explaining how he adapted or evolved his thinking along the way. His stories are relatable because they're not a load of hooey coming from on-high from an "all-knowing" internal-audit God; he is fallible, admits mistakes and missteps, and offers his lessons-learned. These stories lay the foundation for his view of World-Class Internal Audit and explain how he came to have this view."

- "Anyone that is passionate, motivated, and enthusiastic about the internal audit and enterprise risk management profession should read this book!

  "It will inspire you further to strive for continuous improvement, professional development, greater quality of the services you perform, and finally, it will infuse you with greater enthusiasm and determination in the pursuit of a world class internal audit organization."

Norman's blogs are at normanmarks.wordpress.com and https://iaonline.theiia.org/blogs/marks.

Appendix A: Example of a risk management policy – BHP Billiton

The following is the risk management policy[165] of BHP Billiton, a major global resources company based in Australia.

> Risk is inherent in our business. The identification and management of risk is central to delivering on the Corporate Objective.

> Risk will manifest itself in many forms and has the potential to impact the health and safety, environment, community, reputation, regulatory, operational, market and financial performance of the Group and, thereby, the achievement of the Corporate Objective.

> By understanding and managing risk we provide greater certainty and confidence for our shareholders, employees, customers and suppliers, and for the communities in which we operate.

> Successful risk management can be a source of competitive advantage.

> Risks faced by the Group shall be managed on an enterprise-wide basis. The natural diversification in the Group's portfolio of commodities, geographies, currencies, assets and liabilities is a key element in our risk management approach.

> We will use our risk management capabilities to maximise the value from our assets, projects and other business opportunities and to assist us in encouraging enterprise and innovation.

> Risk management will be embedded into our critical business activities, functions and processes. Risk understanding and our tolerance for risk will be key considerations in our decision making.

> Risk issues will be identified, analysed and ranked in a consistent manner. Common systems and methodologies will be used.

---

[165] Available on the Internet, this version of the policy is dated 2009.

Risk controls will be designed and implemented to reasonably assure the achievement of our Corporate Objective.

The effectiveness of these controls will be systematically reviewed and, where necessary, improved.

Risk management performance will be monitored, reviewed and reported. Oversight of the effectiveness of our risk management processes will provide assurance to executive management, the Board and shareholders.

The effective management of risk is vital to the continued growth and success of our Group.

When the policy was issued, it was signed by the company's CEO.

Appendix B: Example of a risk management policy – CQUniversity

The following is from CQUniversity Australia[166]. Its risk management policy is based primarily on ISO 31000:2009.

RISK MANAGEMENT

1 PURPOSE

CQUniversity is committed to the management of risk as an integral part of its operations, focusing on strategies to minimise risks to University mission and objectives.

The objectives of this policy are to:

- outline the University's approach to risk management;
- improve decision-making, accountability and outcomes through the effective use of risk management;
- integrate risk management into daily operations of the University; and
- consider risk appetite in strategic and operational decision making.

2 SCOPE

This policy applies to all areas and staff of the University.

3 EFFECTIVE DATE   6 August 2014

4 LEGISLATIVE AUTHORITY

- Financial Accountability Act 2009 (Qld)
- Financial and Performance Management Standard 2009 (Qld)

---

[166] Included with permission

- Planning and Reporting Policy
- TEQSA Risk Assessment Framework version 2.0
- Work Health and Safety Act 2011 and relevant Regulation and Codes of Practice

5 POLICY STATEMENT

CQUniversity is committed to managing risk in accordance with the process set out in the Australian/New Zealand Joint Standard on Risk Management (AS/NZS ISO 31000:2009) in order to benefit the University and manage the cost of risk. To meet this commitment, risk is to be every employee's business. All employees are required to be responsible and accountable for managing risk in so far as is reasonably practicable within their area of responsibility.

Sound risk management principles and practices must become part of the normal management strategy for all business units within CQUniversity.

The management of risk is to be integrated into CQUniversity's existing planning and operational processes and is to be fully recognised in the University's reporting processes.

6 RESPONSIBILITIES

Compliance, Monitoring and Review

6.1 Vice-Chancellor and President

The Vice-Chancellor and President is accountable to the University Council and has overall responsibility as the 'accountable officer' for protecting the University from unacceptable costs or losses associated with its operations, and for developing and implementing systems for effectively managing the risks that may affect the achievement of objectives and operational outcomes.

6.2 Executive and Senior Management

The effectiveness of risk management is unavoidably linked to management competence, commitment and integrity, all of which forms the basis of sound Corporate Governance. Corporate Governance provides a systematic framework within which the Executive Management group can discharge their duties in managing the University.

Executive and Senior Management are responsible for:

- providing direction and guidance within their areas of accountability so that subordinates best utilise their abilities in the preservation of the University's resources

- successfully promoting, sponsoring and coordinating the development of a risk management culture throughout the University

- guiding the inclusion of risk management in all strategic and operational decision making

- possessing a clear profile of major risks within their area of control incorporating both opportunity and negative risks

- maintaining a framework to manage, monitor and report risk

- managing risks to meet University objectives, goals and vision and

- improving Corporate Governance.

6.3 Line Management

Line Managers at all levels will be responsible for the adoption of risk management practices and will be directly responsible for the results of risk management activities, relevant to their area of responsibility. As part of the annual planning cycle all responsible managers will be required to consider and document existing risks and their impact on proposed plans. Any new risks identified due to changes in the business environment must also be documented. Risk records must be maintained up-to-date on an on-going basis to reflect any changes which may occur.

6.4 All Employees

All employees are responsible for:

- acting at all times in a manner which does not place at risk the health and safety of themselves or any other person in the workplace

- providing direction and training to persons for whom they have a supervisory responsibility or duty of care provision relating to health and safety

- identifying areas where risk management practices should be adopted and are to advise their supervisors accordingly

- meeting their obligations under relevant legislation including Workplace Health and Safety, Equal Employment Opportunity and Anti-Discrimination and

- taking all practical steps to minimise the University's exposure to contractual, tortuous and professional liability.

6.5 Audit, Compliance and Risk Committee

The Committee is responsible for:

- reviewing this document in conjunction with staff of Internal Audit every three years, or sooner where considered necessary. The outcome of this review will be referred to the University Council for approval

- reviewing the University's strategic risk assessment on an annual basis

- reporting annually to the University Council summarising its review and monitoring activities as they relate to oversight of the risk management process. The Committee will also indicate, in its opinion and based on its activities, any significant business risks which remain at an unacceptably high level.

6.6 Support and Advice

Corporate Reporting, Risk and Planning will support the activities of University risk by providing advice and support on risk management

6.7 Education and Training

The Corporate Reporting, Risk and Planning and Health and Safety Office are responsible for the development and provision of risk management awareness training as well as specific training and education programs throughout the University. This training and education is to address the needs of all and employees including Senior Management.

6.8 The internal audit function will support University risk management through periodic independent review of risk management practices and procedures to provide assurance on their efficiency and relevance to the Committee.

6.9 Records Management

All records relevant to this document are to be maintained in a recognised University recordkeeping system.

7 DEFINITIONS

- **Risk Appetite**: organisation's approach to assess and eventually pursue, retain, take or turn away from risk
- **Risk**: the chance of something happening that will have an impact on objectives.
- **Risk Management**: coordinated activities to direct and control an organisation with regard to risk.
- **Risk Tolerance**: The boundaries of risk taking outside of which the organisation is not prepared to venture in the pursuit of its long term objectives.

Made in the USA
Lexington, KY
26 April 2018